CHARACTER
and
COACHING

Building Virtue in
Athletic Programs

John M. Yeager
John N. Buxton

Amy L. Baltzell
Wallace B. Bzdell

DUDE
PUBLISHING

A Division of
National Professional Resources, Inc.
Port Chester, New York

Character and coaching: building virtue in athletic
programs / John M. Yeager ... [et. al.]—1st ed.
p.cm.
Includes bibliographical references.
ISBN 1-887943-48-X

1. Coaching (Athletics)—Moral and ethical aspects.
2. Sports for children—Psychological aspects.
3. Character. 4. Sportsmanship—Study and teaching.

I. Yeager, John M

GV711.C43 2001   796'.07'7
                                        QBI00-957

Cover design by Faith E. Deegan
Book design by David Gates Creative, Tucson, AZ
Pagesetting by The Service Bureau, Alice Bowman, Tucson, AZ

Dude Publishing
A division of National Professional Resources, Inc.
25 South Regent Street
Port Chester, New York 10573
Toll free: (800) 453-7461
Phone: (914) 937-8879

Visit our Web Site: www.nprinc.com

Printed in the United States of America

ISBN 1-887943-48-X

To George Wheeler—
whose spirit lives in those
who played on his teams.

Acknowledgments

We owe many debts of gratitude to those who assisted us in the process of writing this book. Mark Boyea, the Athletic Director at The Montclair Kimberley Academy, and Eric Hartung, a Research Associate at the New England Research Institute and a doctoral candidate at Boston University, have selflessly added the necessary glue to many of the chapters.

This book couldn't have been written without the influence from significant researchers and practitioners in the character and sport field. We thank Jeff Beedy and Tom Zierk of Sports-PLUS and Brenda Light Bredemeier and David Light Shields, co-directors of the Mendelson Center for Sport, Character, and Culture at the University of Notre Dame. Also, we have been motivated by the vision of Jim Thompson, the founder of the Positive Coaching Alliance. We have also learned much from the pioneering work in sport psychology from Terry Orlick, Ken Ravizza, Al Petitpas, Steve Danish and Boston University's Leonard Zaichkowsky.

Boston University's School of Education and the Center for the Advancement of Ethics and Character have provided an opportune climate to learn more about the classical foundations of virtue. We are grateful for our relationships with our mentors and colleagues: Dean Edwin Delattre, Kevin Ryan, Karen Bohlin, Steve Ellenwood, Steve Tigner, Bill Russell, Mary Worlton, John Cheffers, Eileen Sullivan, Richard Nastasi and Phil Tate. Also, we appreciate the thoughts of Jack Parker, the BU hockey coach and Ed Carpenter, BU's Sports Information Director. We thank current BU graduate and former graduate students who aspire to teach character-based education: Cindy Adams, Jerry Larson, John

McCarthy, Lori Ciccomascolo, Mark Catarella, Deborah Farmer, Danielle Cote, Mark Harris, Denny Wright, Adam Naylor, Doug Gardner, Chuck McCormick, and Donna Duffy.

We are grateful to Peter Greer, Bob Bigelow and William Gaine, Jr. for their enlightened views of character and sport. We thank Peter Haberl and Sean McCann of the United States Olympic Training Center for their insights on character and elite athletes.

Although it would take pages to mention the many athletes, coaches and athletic directors who have influenced us, we acknowledge the contributions of Erin Quinn, John Pirani, TJ Williams, Gordon Webb, Kevin Hicks, Carol Kleinfelder, Steve Bristol, Rob Morris, Alan McCoy, Rich Irving, Pat Callahan, Shelagh Donohue, and Tom Campbell.

Most of all, our families deserve much recognition for their support in our endeavors. They are as much a part of this book as we are.

Culver, Indiana
January, 2001

John M.Yeager
John N. Buxton
Amy L. Baltzell
Wallace D. Bzdell

Contents

Introduction

*Sport does not provide us with many answers to the
issues of life, but rather provides us with one of the
richest fields for asking the questions.*
                                                    Drew Hyland

Sport Matters!

Sport matters to us. We realized this when we began the planning
process for the book. We all had significant involvement with sport
—at the youth, high school, Olympic, and professional levels—as
athletes, coaches, and program administrators. We brought to the
table our experiences from the cold outdoor skating rinks in Western Canada, from the hard-rubber wrestling mats in Providence, RI,
from the lacrosse fields of New England, and from the waters of
Boston's Charles River. These venues provided us with the environment to participate in competitive experiences that really mattered, and these experiences were indelibly etched in our minds,
and in some cases, on our bodies as physical reminders. Yes, we
admit it. Sport has helped shape who we are today.

This book is a reflection of the ongoing work of the Character and Sport Initiative (CSI), a program founded at Boston University's Center for the Advancement of Ethics and Character and
now based at the Culver Academies in Culver, Indiana. The CSI
emphasizes the influence of participation on the character formation of all stakeholders in an athletic program—coaches, athletic

directors, parents, officials, athletes, and other important people. The CSI believes that most people participate in sports because it brings them some level of happiness. One of the classic aims of life is for people to aspire to authentic happiness. When a program is managed well, participation offers this opportunity. And, as we all know, the fields and courts can also be the venues for frustration, despair, and in the not-so-rare case, tragedy.

Character Matters!

We also believe that most intelligent people involved in athletics would agree that proper behavior makes the sport better—that **character matters.** Playing by the rules and respecting other participants give people the greatest opportunity to perform well and enjoy the experience. Good character is defined as the formation of and action on universally desirable traits such as respect, responsibility, courage, moderation/balance, care and compassion, trustworthiness, generosity, and humility. However, not every athlete, coach, and parent has formed a good character. As Hayward Hale Broun once said, "Sports do not build character. They reveal it." Arguments will continue regarding the extent to which the playing field can serve as the venue for learning life's lessons. We hope to shed some light on this matter. Whether people believe that participation in sports helps to form character or not, we do know that a healthy atmosphere is essential for providing participants with a genuinely satisfying and enjoyable experience.

The Challenge

Although more people now play in organized athletics than ever before, the number of young people dropping out of programs has increased significantly, as has the number of complaints about inappropriate game behavior by coaches and parents. Also on the increase are the number of parents, coaches, and players who weigh in with an excessive "win at any cost" attitude. For some, sport participation is not the pure, satisfying experience it was intended to be. If people are serious about bringing the purity back, then it's time to conduct business differently. To this end, there has been an evolution of "sportsmanship" programs throughout the United States, intended to heighten awareness about the realities of sport today.

We are concerned that many well-intentioned sportsmanship programs may be missing the mark. Troubled by the superficiality of some "character-based" programs, the Center for Advancement of Ethics and Character established the Character and Sport Initiative to address the complexities involved in influencing the stakeholders in athletic programs.

By overwhelming confirmation, most people involved in athletics say that the "character" piece matters—that every sport is made better when those involved behave properly. This begs an important question. If people believe that sport is such a good thing, why do there seem to be so many problems? Are we doing what we say we are doing with our athletic programs? In others words, if character is important, what are we doing to make it important in reality?

With these questions in mind, we began our journey down a different road—not as athletes or coaches, but now as listeners and observers. In the past two years, we have received generous and enlightening feedback from student-athletes, coaches, parents, and program administrators at the youth, secondary school, and college levels, as well as the elite levels of organized sports. Comments from these individuals confirmed something that we already suspected—that many heads of school (principals, athletic directors, and coaches) want practical strategies that directly address the issue of character in their programs.

We have come to realize two other important things. First, a more explicit or specific approach is needed in which program stakeholders declare what matters most in their athletic program. In other words, many coaches, parents, athletic directors, and school heads say that "good character" and "sportsmanship" are

...portant, but fail to back up this belief in the structure and mission of their programs. We have found that many of the adults who are involved in well-meaning and well-intentioned athletic programs are not willing to take the time, energy, resources, and finances necessary to create, implement, and maintain a character-based athletic program. They are content to continue functioning with a "damage-control" mentality. Lots of talk, but not enough action!

Second the relationship between character and performance is seldom addressed. Most coaches are in the business of human performance. This can't be ignored. However, many coaches separate the character piece from the actual strategy and task on the field. We believe, as many of you do, that the two are vitally interconnected. Most people involved in a sport strive to win. Regardless of winning or losing, a person's character should remain the same. It is the foundation of all human behavior. Despite the logical link between character and performance, many coaches continue to consider the myth that paying too much attention to the athletes' character will soften their focus on performance.

The Solution: A Practical Guide

This book is a practical guide that supports coaches, administrators, and organizers of athletic programs in understanding the true nature of the challenge. Similar to the development of a coach's well-thought-out practice plan, this book addresses five concepts that form an integrated model to help all the stakeholders realize the potential benefits of participation in athletic programs.

① *Personal History*

Program stakeholders' past sport experiences may have a strong influence on how they teach their children and coach their athletes. Adults must take time to reflect thoughtfully on their own experiences in order to understand the "why" of their values and behavior.

② Walking the Talk

We believe that modeling good behavior—to lead by deed—is an important way to influence young people's character development. When sport participants see their coaches, parents, and mentors "walking the talk," they will realize that the commitment to ideals is genuine.

③ Partnership

There must be an ongoing partnership among school administrators, parents, and coaches regarding the character development of athletes. While parents are the prime character educators, all adults associated with the athletic program must embody and reflect the moral authority invested in them.

④ Accepting Responsibility

All those who work with young people must make an effort to identify opportunities for positive modeling and growth. They also should work to create and identify the responsibilities they have to develop each athlete's character.

⑤ Evaluation

Those responsible for the athletic program need to stress the importance of the evaluation of these activities. Changing habits, developing and reinforcing good behavior, and establishing standards of right and wrong action all take time. Those who are serious about doing well by young people must be willing to measure the reality of their progress against their best intentions.

Any game is played at various levels, physical as well as mental. At the highest level, all participants are challenged to fulfill the principles in these five tenets. We all need to step over the line and onto the playing field at this level, becoming actively involved in reflecting on own experiences, building partnerships, accepting responsibility, evaluating the programs, and —most importantly—in walking the talk.

Coaches have written this book for all adults who have influence on athletic programs. It cuts to the core of the impact that good coaching has on the character formation of athletes. Through examination of the underlying purposes of sport and the need to establish common ground with other coaches, program directors, parents, and athletes, *Character and Coaching* provides the basis for programs that are founded on respect, tradition, and success at all levels. Coaches will begin to assess their own sport experiences and learn to apply practical, hands-on strategies that can make a difference with their athletes and their programs. They will find in these pages a solid, researched, and informed foundation on which to build the athletic program they all want as mentors of athletes.

Character and Coaching is a primer that will allow coaches to put the "character" questions into a useable context, using language that encourages all those who are working with young people to put those things first which matter most. *Character and Coaching* introduces a straightforward and sports-based context that serves as a foundation on which coaches can put the lessons of character coaching to use.

Although parents are the major moral educators of their children, coaches and athletic directors also influence character development through both their words and their actions. This book challenges coaches, athletic directors, and parents to know, value, and act on the core virtues of their athletic programs. Virtues are universally desirable characteristics that we would expect all stakeholders to exhibit on the playing field.

Some individuals say that people take sport too seriously. We believe if participation in sport influences character, then sport isn't taken seriously enough. If it were, we wouldn't see many of the problems currently associated with it. The easy question to ask is whether sport builds or merely reveals character. In order to take sport seriously, we must ask people to declare what matters most to them. This question is essential.

Asking the Right Questions

Although this book provides strategies for creating or modifying a "character" game plan in athletic programs, it also asks the tough questions of the well-meaning and well-intentioned adults who influence the program.

All coaches understand the tendency to focus on what matters most to them. Most coaches realize that the psychological and physical well being of the young people in their care is their highest priority. However, the underlying purpose of sport seldom enters the conversation. Coaches end up constantly debating X's and O's—offense vs. defense, fundamentals vs. strategies—rather than addressing the more essential questions: *Why are we doing this in the first place? Who benefits from all this work? Are we actually making a difference with our athletes?*

Every good education begins with a question. So we challenge you, first by asking you to focus on important questions, rather than quick-fix solutions and answers. We already know those answers. We have our own experiences to inform us about that. Factors such as lack of motivation, lack of work ethic, and unprincipled coaches, as well as inconsistent messages from parents, coaches, and important others influence enjoyment and satisfaction in sport. We know about it, but what do we *do* about it?

Character and Coaching embraces the philosophical, psychological, and educational foundations of the relationship between character and sport. It gives the coach and athletic director theoretical and practical instruction on how to create, implement, and maintain a character-based athletic program. The program is presented in a style that is accessible to all coaches. It is divided into three sections that provide clear, understandable explanations of terms, concepts, and practical methodologies that coaches can capture, then reflect on, and put into action.

Section 1—Awareness

Chapter 1: Reclaiming the Purpose of Sport. This chapter is designed to help coaches and athletic directors examine their own motivations and purposes in sport. The central question is this:

- What are the aims of sport participation?

Chapter 2: Establishing Common Ground. When there is common ground among participants, the program sends a more consistent message to the athletes. This chapter examines the foundations of character education and defines those character habits that support the establishment of common ground among those working with student-athletes. Two questions are important:

- What are character habits and how do they relate to sport?

- How do we establish common ground with others on the definitions of character habits?

Chapter 3: Coach as Character Educator. Coaches can be a significant influence in student-athletes' overall development. By appropriate mentoring, modeling, and managing, good coaches can reinforce habits of good character with their athletes. The question is this:

- What are the responsibilities and opportunities of coaches as character educators?

Section 2—Assessment

Chapter 4: Discovering the Joy of Sport Throughout the Life Span. Here we look at how coaches and athletic directors can self-evaluate their own sport experience and reflect on how these experiences influence the work they do with student-athletes. The critical question is as follows:

- How have our own sport experiences influenced us as adult mentors?

Chapter 5: Identifying the Formal Structure of Teams/ Programs. This chapter shows how coaches and athletic directors can complete a snapshot assessment of their own team/program core virtues and evaluate areas of improvement in the delivery of high quality, character-rich service to the student-athletes. Two questions are important:

- Who are the stakeholders that influence your athletic program?

- What are the competing motivations among them?

Chapter 6: Identifying Team and Program Core Virtues. This chapter demonstrates how coaches and athletic directors identify team/program core virtues and competing motivations. Three questions need to be asked:

- What would you want other people to say about your team or athletic program?

- Are your team and program core virtues in alignment with the ideal? Are we doing what we say we are doing?

- If not, what needs to be done to bring them into alignment?

Section 3—Application

Chapter 7: Walking the Talk: Building Core Virtues in Athletic Programs. Here we explain how coaches and athletic directors can learn how to apply core virtues in the athletic program by creating and/or modifying their school's or program's mission statement. Three questions need to be addressed:

- Is your program mission clearly defined and specific?

- Is the mission consistently carried out?

- What does the mission look like in action?

Chapter 8: Walking the Talk II: Character Links to Perfor- mance. This chapter provides instruction on practical strategies that help coaches link character habits to excellence on the field.

It also emphasizes the importance of self-monitoring activities in helping coaches model appropriate behavior when working with student-athletes. One question is paramount:

- How are your program's core virtues connected to performance on the field?

Chapter 9: Next Steps: Expanding the Influence of Good character in Sport. Consistently modeling good behavior—leading by deed—is essential. Developing good character, like acquiring a sport skill, requires hard work, consistent and faithful practice, patience, perseverance, constant striving for improvement, and respect for the advice of knowledgeable and consistent coaches, athletic directors, and parents. One essential question is:

- What does the plan for a character-based athletic program look like in action?

During our travels, a compelling phrase from an airline magazine advertisement for Deloitte Consulting, Inc. caught our attention. We thought the quote would be an appropriate wrap-up for our introduction and an excellent way of leading into Chapter 1.

"Strategies deliver promises.
People and processes deliver results."

Awareness

Reclaiming the Purpose of Sport

All human activities aim at some good:
Some goods subordinate to others.
Aristotle — *The Nichomachean Ethics*

Sport as a Vehicle for Happiness

I frequently bring my young daughter to the playground adjacent to the high school fields I once played and coached on. As I push her on the swing, I take a panoramic view of the fields that once provided me with joy, elation and sometimes, frustration. So many thoughts and memories of practices and games come to mind. These are recollections of a time past; the fields are empty now. It is quiet, except for the squeaky chain-link of the swing supporting the weight and momentum of my daughter happily flying through the air without a care in the world.

As I stand beside the swing, I look to my right and reflect on the electric scoreboard, which was dedicated in the memory of George Wheeler, my beloved high school soccer coach. For those who knew George, the last thing he would want dedicated to his memory was a scoreboard. An appropriate epitaph would mention something about the way he was able to impress his players to strive to perform their best while respecting the essence of the game. The final scores — the wins and losses — were woven together with something more important — the character formation of his players. That's what really mattered to him.

I remember the cold October day in 1970 when, as a varsity soccer goalkeeper, I painfully misjudged a 30-yard clearing kick by the league-leading opposing team. As I lost the ball in sun, it went sailing over my head into the back of the net. We lost, 1–0, one of the best games I ever played; except for that one major mistake. I remember going to see George in his office after I showered. I was ashamed of my mistake and wanted to apologize to him for letting him and the team down. He surprised me. "Yeags, what a great day it was." (I'm not sure where he found that nickname for me, but it certainly has stuck). "Of course," he went on to say, "I'm disappointed with the final outcome as I know you are, too. But what a wonderful opportunity we had today! For most of the game, we played the second best team in the state to a 0–0 tie."

This was how George looked at sport—making a wealth of opportunities available to all student-athletes. So when I return my energies to the swing set and my happy daughter, I look to the George Wheeler Memorial Scoreboard and think how grateful I am for the value of his mentoring. He helped me aspire to know the good, value the good, and act on the good. Besides that 1–0 loss, I don't remember any other scores of soccer games that I played or coached under him, but George Wheeler's teams won a lot more games than they lost. However, I remember everything about what mattered to him. I miss him dearly, but his spirit lives on in my life and the other lives he has touched. —John Yeager

Sport has provided many of us with important experiences in our lives. We often recall those experiences, whether on a cold October afternoon in the final days of the fall sports season, or on a morning in late February, when a premature thaw (typical in New England) announces that the spring season is close by.

But sport is not only about the seasons, nor is it only about the fields, the courts, the ice, and the pools. They are not the game. The sticks, helmets, bats, balls, and goals are not the game. What the game should be is a healthy interaction, a balance of competition and cooperation of well-intentioned human beings. The equipment is merely a prop.

Erin Quinn, a lacrosse and football coach at Middlebury College, once said that lacrosse, in and of itself, means very little when you take the people out of the equation. It is the collaboration of players, coaches, officials, athletic and program directors, parents, and other important people in addition to the application of one's own efforts that brings meaning to the game. That collaboration can foster relationships and build friendships —and many of us cherish the friendships that have developed as a result. But sport also provides everyone involved with opportunity to develop his or her own character. We have had the opportunity, as many of you have had, to meet a great number of people who share this love of sport, not just for the joy of the game, but also for how the game has helped us develop as human beings.

Sport as Positive Experience—Doing Right by Sport

Sport means different things to different people. Although the purposes of sport are numerous, most theorists and enthusiasts would agree that physical activity and sport participation can be intrinsically valuable. We learn the joy of movement, the challenge of taking risks. We learn something about our limitations as well as our strengths. We learn to work cooperatively toward a common goal. We learn the importance of teamwork. We build our communications skills. We develop or reinforce confidence, trust, and humility. And if we weren't very confident, trustworthy, and humble before we started playing, maybe we learned a little about these qualities on the field.

The activities of play and sport may teach us something about virtue, which can lead to and reinforce the habits of good character—habits that equate with just and right actions in life. From the time children first begin to explore their physical world to the moment athletes engage in competition, individuals experience situations that provide opportunities for personal growth. While play develops the child's sense of exploration and independence, sport fosters the spirit of collaboration and competition.

However, there is always a risk of contamination by well-meaning and well-intentioned adults who mistakenly make more out of sport than should be made. The adults—coaches and parents—hold the role of the official organizers. They set the guidelines. They model appropriate (or inappropriate) behavior on and off the field. This behavior influences the young people in their charge.

It is important for all of us to believe that our knowledge of sport, our values, and our personal goals are strong and pure enough to allow us, individually and collectively, to dialogue with other coaches and parents, even those whose thinking and perspective on sport are not in the best interests of the young people in their mutual care. Many young people are participating in organized athletics as early as age three. They are being exposed to a variety of adult mentors. In some cases, by the time these advanced toddlers have become adolescents, they have played over 2,000 games and have either been educated by responsible adult coaches or contaminated by self-serving adults. Many high school coaches welcome freshmen student-athletes with over ten years of structured athletic experience. Unfortunately, some young people never get to this place, because they decided to stop playing in organized sports by age thirteen or fourteen—disillusioned by unfulfilled expectations and misguided mentors. If most people agree that sport participation ought to be a joyful, lasting experience, why are many adult mentors missing the mark with so many of our young people?

We believe that it is essential to examine the responsibilities and opportunities coaches have in the education and development of the young people in their care. In what ways can coaches, athletic directors, and parents identify and support those core virtues that are available through the joyful experience of sport? The formation of good character, like the acquisition of an athletic skill, requires a solid work ethic, perseverance, and self-discipline, as well as respect for self, opponents, and teammates. These traits are the by-products of well-intentioned young people working with self-confident and appropriately reflective adults who have challenged themselves to reach their full potential as mentors.

William Russell, former co-director of Boston University's Center for the Advancement of Ethics and Character, suggests that "as the aim in any sport is for a participant to apply skills along with the development of habits which make a desired move automatic and second nature, so, too, the aim of character formation is the acquisition of those habits of thinking, feeling, and acting that demonstrate the abiding virtues which reveal good character. Put another way, the aim is to develop habits around knowing the good, loving the good and doing the good. The kind of degree of hard effort is similar in both the formation of an athletic skill and a character habit."

To ensure that our children and athletes enjoy the positive experience available in sport, we need to remember that character is influenced by many sources. Parents, teachers, peers, coaches, and other role models work interdependently to reinforce the virtues we call integrity and justice. All must acknowledge the responsibilities and opportunities they have to educate and develop the young people in their care.

As adults, all of us are challenged to step over that imaginary line that separates our normal observation of a sport from an active mental involvement in which we examine our own attitudes and experiences through thoughtful reflection to ensure that our motives and actions are pure. And when we believe that our motives are pure, we need to act on those beliefs—our actions speak as loudly as our words.

The Major Adult Stakeholders in the Sport Experience

Coaches

Along with the responsibilities of coaching and mentoring come the opportunities for joy, satisfaction, frustration, and elation. Many coaches still become exhilarated every time they step on the practice or game field. For some coaches, the playing environment represents a sacred shrine, an ideal, an emotional outlet and, usually, a learning experience. Most importantly, it represents not only a responsibility, but also a unique opportunity. Like the athlete, the coach takes a risk once he or she steps on the game field. That risk is created by the many factors and influences he or she cannot control—and for many coaches, it is precisely this risk that creates the excitement. The noted sports philosopher, Drew Hyland, claims that there is always some degree of doubt or anticipation regarding the process and outcome of the game. When you come to the field, in whatever capacity—coach, athlete, parent, official—you step over that line and invite yourself into a process without being exactly sure how the event will turn out. That is the risk we take.

The bottom line is having to commit or declare oneself to the process. Hyland also suggests that stepping over the line is an opportunity to try to make oneself "more complete;" that many people believe that playing or coaching somehow gives them a chance to become "whole." This may be seen in the incredible elation experienced by a coach who witnesses the fruits of his or her hard work; only to have that feeling replaced two days later with a sense of hopelessness when his or her team turns in a sub-par performance. The question is whether the need to be whole can also be viewed as a positive motivation or as a deficit situation which must be controlled.

Many intangibles influence the sport experience. Coaches can't control the level of preparation of the other team. They can't control the physical environment: a soggy field, an unmowed infield, soft ice, a cold swimming pool, or a soft mat. However, good mentors are capable of controlling their players' actions on the field. Some days everything seems to go perfectly —everything fits into place. On other days coaches are reminded of the phrase, "We didn't show up today!"

Although most players and coaches walk onto the field in a physical condition similar to their physical condition during a previous game or practice, their mental preparation may be quite different. Imagine the thoughts that went through the U.S. Olympic Speedskating team's coaches at the 1988 Winter Olympics in Calgary. Many people remember watching the then current world champion speedskater, Dan Jansen, fall coming around the final turn in the 500 meter race. Knowing that his sister had died that morning most certainly had an influence on his concentration and ultimately his performance. Most coaches and athletes are exposed to much less traumatic and dramatic stimuli every day, but their issues still influence how they attend to what matters on the field.

Parents

Every time parents attend their children's games, either at the youth, high school, college, or even Olympic level; they also take a risk. We have interviewed many proud Moms and Dads who remark that it is difficult to see the whole field when their child is out there. It is understandable that it may be challenging to watch everything else that is happening when you are heavily invested in the well being of your child, as all good parents ought to be. Parents, for the most part, want the best for their children.

Once the whistle blows the anticipation intensifies. There are many people involved in the game who have the opportunity to influence the process and the outcome. This includes a son's or daughter's chance for satisfaction and enjoyment. This can become highly stressful for some parents who believe they must take a more active role in their child's game. Whether it is by constructive applause and rooting or coercive booing, the parent influences the process. It is essential for us, as adults, to remember that our main purpose is to act in a manner that promotes the well being of the young people playing on the field; that the experience is primarily about and for the children or adolescents who are playing the game.

Officials

Another group of adults merits mention. The person who blows the whistle is also an integral part of the competitive and collaborative process. Officials have two main responsibilities: (1) they make judgment calls based on the play of the game; and (2) they oversee the code of conduct for a particular sport. However, this process cannot be achieved in a vacuum. As other "stakeholders" in the process, officials are human and, therefore, fallible. They ought to be viewed as working in partnership, in a collaborative effort with the coaches to help make the game better for the players.

Coaches, parents, and officials are the stakeholders that provide the structure for the sport, so an athlete's responsibilities and opportunities can be showcased in a practice or a game. It is the chance for the joy of movement in a social setting that allows for young people to grow. It is the stepping over the line that invites us into a collaborative effort. It's about the young people, but note that all are there to experience the benefits of sport, and each deserves to be treated with respect by the other participants.

Competition and Collaboration—The Ideal of Sport

It is essential to remember that every time you step onto the field, you become another "part of the whole" of the collective sport experience. This is a collaboration of teammates, the opposing team and staff/coaches, officials, athletic directors, parents and other spectators. It stands to reason that if one team doesn't show up, either in reality or in by performing poorly, the game is compromised. If the official doesn't show up, somebody must fill in or there is no game. Also, if parents and other spectators don't attend, the game becomes a very different kind of event.

This actually happened several years ago at a Division I men's college basketball game. Several players on the visiting team had come down with the measles. Both teams and staff were immunized as a result. However, as a preventive health measure, health officials mandated that only essential team personnel attend the game. The game was still played, and only a select few could hear the echo of each bounce of the ball on the floor or swish through the basket. The teams still played hard, but no one knows what the cost was to the quality or outcome of the game.

It is not uncommon in league schedules to have strongly talented teams playing against much weaker ones. However, a 30–0 blowout doesn't serve anybody well. Recently, the commissioner of a northeastern United States city high school league was chastised for calling in inaccurate scores for some of the school's hockey games to the metropolitan newspaper. When challenged by this manipulation, the commissioner stated that he didn't want to bruise the losing team's self-esteem by providing the lopsided scores in print.

This situation parallels a comment that Jack Parker, the well respected and legendary men's hockey coach at Boston University, made at a recent conference. He mentioned that he had chatted with a couple of youth hockey players who were going on the ice with their team after Boston University's practice one day. Coach Parker asked them how their season was going. One proud boy exclaimed, "Great! We're 73 and 5." Jack was taken aback and with little reflection, realized that if one team enjoyed a 73–5 record, there might well be another team at 5–73.

The inequity of talent on different teams at different schools will continue to be responsible for occasional routs and blowouts. However, many athletic organizations are attempting to bring some parity to their programs and leagues. Regardless of talent, good coaches ought to make sure that their team's practices and games reflect a sense of collaboration that ensures not only striving for good performance, but leaves a sense of satisfaction and enjoyment. We are not quite sure that a score in a large newspaper is going to influence an adolescent's sense of self-worth as much as the opportunities made available by his or her coach who finds ways to ensure some sense of success on the ice whether the score is 4–3 or 18–0.

This sense of satisfaction can happen individually in striving to do one's best. It can also happen only when there is an opponent to compete against. In game situations, many coaches treat the opposing team, and possibly the officials, as obstacles. The respect that ought to be accorded to opposing teams is, what Drew Hyland calls, "the necessity of the opponent." The interdependent relationship that occurs can be a mutually beneficial experience. The opponent must be involved for the game to take place.

The CSI staff recently listened to a youth soccer coach on a local radio call-in show recall the wonderful experience of his team playing in a weekend tournament and making it to the finals. The championship game went into overtime and then into penalty kicks. His team lost in the third round of penalty kicks. He said it was the most exciting thing to see two evenly matched teams, head to head, kick for kick. Most coaches and athletes have few experiences in which this collaboration brings out the best in performance and attitude. The nature of the collaboration, one team pushing the other, brought out the best in all the players and both teams came away from the experience with a fresh sense of accomplishment and genuine satisfaction. From a different angle of vision, the members of the winning team in a vigorously contested game ought to, in an appropriate manner, congratulate the loser for pushing them to play better. This suggestion for some is preposterous. However, upon reflection, it represents the importance of the opponent—the collaborative value of the contest.

Peter Haberl, the sport psychology consultant for the United States women's hockey team that won the gold medal in Nagano, Japan, in 1998, relates the collaborative approach that the team's head coach, Ben Smith, takes. He said that Ben also knows that, at this level, he needs to win (or he's not coming back). "His job depends on it. . . . That motivates him, and that's why I like working with him," Peter told us, then went on to recall one thing Smith said to the U.S. team before the final game—repeating a point he emphasized in January when they were on the road. "Ben said, in essence, that he wanted the Canadians to play

really, really well in the final. He then said to the playe
we are going to play a little bit better.' He brings the n
that they are going to help us play better ourselves." (A more
detailed account of Ben's philosophy appears in Mary Turco's
Crashing the Net, the definitive documentary of the U.S. women's
hockey team's quest for gold.)

Sport is made better when competition and collaboration
are appropriately balanced. True, competition, in and of itself,
can be a very healthy process. It can be a wonderful experience.
But when the whistle blows—and this team and that team meet
—there is also a collaborative experience. There is an integration
of teams, coaches, spectators, and officials. Competition and collaboration merge.

Most of you have had several moments of participation
when "all the planets were aligned," competition and collaboration were in balance, and the experience was joyful, fulfilling,
and enduring. And you will never forget that day. The memory
of those moments still drive you to do what you do in sport.

Conflict in Sport

Therefore, healthy competition makes for a collaborative experience. Many dictionaries will state that competition is a "striving
or vying with another or others for profit, prize, position, or the
necessities of life; rivalry. A contest, match or other trial of skill
or ability." The risks and challenges associated with the competitive sport process can bring joy, frustration, and elation. However,
striving to perform well can invite obsessive, selfish behavior without regard for others involved. This, as most of us are keenly
aware, can cause problems. Taking sport too seriously introduces
the possibility of disappointment and unfulfilled expectations.

Occasionally, the competitive atmosphere is contaminated
by the actions of either a player, coach, parent, or official.
Although these actions may seem to be unintentional, a slightly

misguided action may cause a problem for someone else. How does that fit into the idea of character formation, and how do character and sport influence each other within that process? When this happens, it is not competition as we would like to know it to be—it is conflict!

We are not talking only about when the conflict leads to a physical injury. We are talking about when the soul of a seven-year-old, or a fifteen-year-old, or a twenty-year-old is injured. That's conflictual. Who is responsible for this action? It is typically an adult who has lost control of the situation. However, we are all fallible and conflict occasionally happens on the field or behind the scenes, but we ought to keep these misguided actions or omissions to a minimum. We must make sure that those responsible for overseeing this behavior are fulfilling their obligations.

When competition becomes so fierce and intense that young people are unnecessarily hurt, whether it be physically, emotionally, mentally, socially, or spiritually (loss of purpose and meaning for sport participation), the game becomes a conflictual, not competitive experience. Although we teach our young people to deal with conflict, we don't have to create additional conflict for them. There is enough conflict in the world today. Subtle antagonistic taunting, referee bashing, and the berating of players is selfish and unacceptable.

John Corlett, of the University of Ottawa, paints a compelling illustration about the potential for conflict in sport in his article entitled, "The Red Queen Effect: Avoiding Life's Treadmill." Corlett quotes the character of the Red Queen in Lewis Carroll's *Through the Looking Glass*.

> *The Red Queen says to Alice that "it takes all the running you can do to keep in the same place. If you want to get somewhere else, you must run at least twice as fast as that!"*

This may sound all too familiar to adults, who also happen to coach and live a frenetic, Type A, fast-paced life. Corlett draws an important parallel from what the Red Queen says. He claims that:

In biology, the evolution of relationships that evolve between predators and their prey has been known as the Red Queen effect. Any adaptation in a prey species is matched in subsequent generations by counter-adaptations in predator species. As the hunted become faster and more agile, so are those that hunt them. This arms race escalates in perpetuity, with neither side ever able to gain sufficient advantage to be safe from the threat of being eaten or starved to extinction. Athletes are used to the Red Queen effect. They train to become stronger, faster, and more skilled, knowing that other athletes are doing the same. Their coaches devise new strategies, knowing that other coaches will find ways to render them obsolete. Most athletes end their careers knowing that they were defeated at least as many times as they were victorious, a clear indication of the red queen effect dictating the nature of the competitive culture.

Corlett claims that in living in this type of culture, it is nearly impossible to get ahead. Living in an outcome/performance based world all of the time welcomes frequent frustration and a continuous struggle to find completeness. Therefore, it is essential to look at the process.

All players ought to be given equal opportunity to improve their skills through participation and the efforts of the coaches. Players at the youth and secondary level are too young to be given up on. Winning at this level should be prioritized in the best interests of the young people, not the adult coaches who do not need to vicariously realize their dreams through their players. In their nation's history of lacrosse, entitled *Tewaarthon*, the Akwesasne Mohawks of upstate New York articulate a guiding principle of the sport: "Our grandfathers told us that when lacrosse was a pure game and was played for the enjoyment of the great spirit, everyone was important, no matter how big or how small, or how strong or how weak." It is evident that the thrill of winning held not such an important role as did how the team played.

Many coaches do not apply Vince Lombardi's quote "winning isn't everything, it's the only thing" appropriately. It is frequently taken out of context, suggesting that winning is a product, and the product is all that matters. Instead, Lombardi's intention was to suggest that striving to win is essential in competition. It is a fact that 50 percent of the teams that compete will lose in any given game (excluding ties). How do we best live knowing that it is inevitable that someone will lose each time there is a game? How much does the final outcome of the game influence our lives? Does the final outcome represent who we are as people?

There ought to be an ongoing partnership between schools, athletic programs, and parents to ensure the realization of the true purpose of sport. Coaches and parents are central to this enterprise and must be educated so that they teach young athletes properly. Not all coaches are professional educators. Even if they haven't all studied the social psychology of children and adolescents, it is very important that their mission is as pure as possible. In others words, they are involved to help and teach young people.

Regardless of established rules and guidelines, acting on the rules and guidelines is essential. We take seriously the actions of those who prevent student-athletes from enjoying the benefits of sport. Therefore, it is essential for dialogue at all the levels of sport, and the dialogue should be aimed at establishing common ground in sport participation. When this happens, the answers to the questions are uncommonly simple, yet very profound and compelling—know what is right action, value it, and act upon it!

And just as in a Shakespearean play, a lot of things happen at a lot of different levels during a game. More often than not, the atmosphere is charged with excitement and anticipation. When you put a bunch of people on the field, it comes alive. Many of us greatly anticipate those moments while sharing a panoramic view of an empty field, gymnasium, or pool.

I still bring my daughter to the playground. I look over at the sun-baked fields during a mid-summer's day—just waiting to come alive. I smile—knowing that preseason practice for the high school soccer team is right around the corner. Will she choose to play soccer and be out there on that field someday? If she does, will it be a satisfying and enjoyable experience for her?

(2)

Establishing Common Ground— Character Formation and Core Virtues

Sow a thought and you reap an act;
Sow an act and you reap a habit;
Sow a habit and you reap a character;
Sow a character and your reap a destiny.
—William Makepeace Thackery

A secondary school's post-season hockey game had ended in melee when a member of the losing team took a swing at one of the other team's players. The association's rules clearly say that all players involved in the fight—regardless of who started it—should be suspended. The coaches for the winning team are engaged in a spirited discussion regarding whether the school should accept or appeal the suspension.

Two coaches are debating the merits of the travel teams in the youth soccer program in their town. They are specifically speaking about a member of the ten-and-under travel team, a nine-year-old girl who is seeing very little playing time. She is not sure if she wants to stay with the team.

What are the correct moral decisions in these situations? Each of these scenarios offers its own nuances. And, as in a sports radio talk show, adult combatants frequently square off on the issues, and in most cases fervently protect their own motives, appetites, and desires.

If the adult mentors who were in charge of these teams had established some common ground on the expectations and core virtues for their respective athletic programs, the right and just answers might have been clearer, the situations less volatile. By expectations, we mean those common assumptions that make the competition possible—for example, that everyone will play by the rules, and that everyone will demonstrate a degree of respect for teammates, opponents, and officials. By core virtues, we mean a consensus of the positive character habits that matter most to those involved in an athletic program.

Reaching consensus on these matters is not always easy. Consequently, it is essential that all concerned have a vehicle for forming an understanding and general agreement on (1) the behaviors that are expected on the field; and (2) a common language that defines actions of good character and that keeps everyone aware of what really matters. When adults use words such as *respect, responsibility, courage,* and *balance* in the context of a practice session or game, they ought to be certain that the athletes understand the meaning and intention behind these words. When we give clear and consistent age-appropriate messages to the athletes in our care, there is a greater likelihood that they will be inspired to act in an acceptable manner. When we establish common ground, players as well as coaches and parents understand the behavioral expectations of participation. When we tell athletes to be respectful and caring to others, and then see a parent or coach not treating the players (on either team) with respect or care through his or her actions, the message becomes confusing.

A coach's voice raised in anger and disapproval, the disappointed look in a parent's eyes, a player angrily kicking the dirt— these actions amplify the confusion. We clearly need to establish agreement on common behavioral definitions of "what right action is" in sport, to develop a set of core virtues from which everyone can work.

This is no easy task. As explained in Chapter 1, people are motivated by many different purposes in sport. If we cannot reach a consensus regarding "what right action is" on the playing field, we set the stage for organizational problems. Getting the majority of, if not all, adults on the same page is essential. All the coaches, athletes, program directors, and parents intersect on the playing field with varied levels of their own character formation. The core virtues of the program must be clear, so each stakeholder knows what behavior is expected of him or her.

The CSI staff has had several conversations with T. J. Williams, the athletic director at Newton North High School in Massachusetts. In the past decade, his teams have collaborated to win several Dalton Trophies, symbolic of competitive excellence on the field as measured by overall league championships. When he was introduced to a group of coaches and athletic directors who envied these accomplishments, he was quick to point out that the remarkable win-loss records and league championships are only a by-product of establishing common ground within the community. This common ground is presented in a twenty-five page manual, created during a three-year process that he compares to the administrative equivalent of eating tin foil. Getting our athletes to follow guidelines is not always easy. Getting adults to find consistency and agreement over policy can really be a struggle.

Defining Core Virtues and Character

The Newton North athletic department handbook (like all good handbooks) is more than words and sentences about playing competitively. It is also founded on actions of good character. What is character? What do these words we call *core values, character habits,* or *virtues* mean operationally? How can they best be put into action?

First, a person's character is the formation of universally desirable traits such as respect and responsibility. It is inevitable that we all develop character, sound or weak. Our moral compasses have been shaped through modeling the behavior of parents and other important people; through moral discussion with parents, coaches, and teachers; and through receiving or avoiding the consequences of certain actions. This type of education begins prior to the child stepping onto the athletic field. In fact, the process of character formation begins immediately after birth in the presence of an infant's caregivers. A person of good character knows the good, loves the good, and does the good. The good, like the Golden Rule, asks us to behave in the manner in which we expect to be treated by others.

Second, it is important for a coach to share understandable and attainable goals, progressive and sequential skill drills, and consistent terminology with his or her team. It is just as essential to ensure that the language used when associating the influence of character in sport is simple for parents, athletic directors, coaches, and players to understand. This terminology commonly includes the virtues that Aristotle talked about 2400 years ago. He never booted up a computer, never drove a car, but his maxims have endured the test of time and are frequently heard on today's playing fields. He observed, in the interrelationship of human beings, the importance of establishing a code of right and wrong. This included the cardinal virtues of wisdom, courage, moderation and justice. These habits can be further divided into associated or allied virtues such as integrity, self-discipline, and caring and compassion. There are many other virtues that may be interchanged. For purposes of this book, we will discuss integrity, justice, courage, moderation, and care and compassion.

Aristotle was interested in the notion that a major goal in life is to aspire to happiness. He believed that this translated to excellence of activity. When people do things well by living a virtuous life, it brings them more happiness. Virtue is for the sake of what kind of person you are; what kind of person you will become. Virtue is about doing the right thing. It is about being a good person. It is about "the flourishing athlete and coach." It is about being treated whole. Although it is highly unlikely that all human beings agree on a "universal or absolute good," that is, right action for all people, it is important to aspire to some level of common ground that has a foundation in creeds, cultures, and communities throughout the world.

Third, when making decisions on or off the playing field, people act with regard to their intellect, feelings, and desires. The nature of one's character determines the precise behavior. If a person has a weakly formed character, the calculative aspect of the intellect will probably focus on self-serving matters–what's in it for me, instead of the intentions of planning to do the right and just action. If a person has a well-formed character, he or she will most likely aspire to act in a consistent, just, and caring manner.

Views, Values, and Virtues

Let's return to the two scenarios introduced at the beginning of this chapter and reduce each to a basic question:

- *Should the suspended hockey players be allowed to play in the next playoff game?*
- *If the soccer player isn't getting playing time, why should she stay on the travel team?*

These types of conflict eventually filter into most sport programs. Often, they embody what we consider to be multi-level conflicts: conflicts of views, values, and virtues.

It is our belief that virtuous behavior serves as a foundation for good action in sport. As we reflect on the various programs we have observed in our travels, we have become very much aware that people's views and values are not necessarily based on virtue. Highly charged views (based on self-interest) and questionable values (based on individual thoughts and feelings) can sometimes be disguised as virtuous behavior. Therefore, it is imperative that we understand the differences between views, values, and virtues through a framework developed by leading character educators, Kevin Ryan and Karen Bohlin.

Views

Many adult sport participants have strong opinions about sport. It would be safe to say that most people who step onto the playing field—coaches, athletes, parents, officials—regard the experience from their own perspective. Controversies among sport stakeholders may often be driven by self-interest, and there is a wide range of compelling arguments about the social issues involved in sport. It is common to have many points of view about any given issue. What some people believe to be most important about sport participation may differ and may be in conflict with one another.

VIEWS are beliefs and opinions that come from an intellectual standpoint. They do not necessarily transmit to behavior. Views may or may not be moral/ethical.

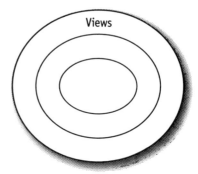

Kevin Ryan and Karen Bohlin, in *Building Character in Schools,* state that "there is nothing wrong with generating controversy in the careful pursuit of the truth. Controversy can prompt reflection, thought, and insight—but it can also provoke anger, resentment, and a contentious spirit that spills out of control." For example, views regarding sport issues are typically expressed in "knock-down, drag-out arguments" where those involved take sides. There is usually a person who plays the role of referee, whose main concern is keeping the process civil and allowing the participants to voice their opinion.

At the end of these typically active conversations, the parties go their separate ways with no healthy resolution to the situation. Ryan and Bohlin would say, "Some subjects end up generating more heat than light."

Values

For purposes of thoughtful reflection, it is essential to distinguish between views and values. Values are things we desire, appetites that we individually prize or regard as worthy. For example, each one of us values different aspects of sport participation. However similar we are, each of us brings our individual interpretation of sport's worth to the field. One person may value winning at any cost, while another values the collaborative interaction of opponents playing in a tightly contested game. Any single individual's values regarding right action in sport may be similar or very different from others.

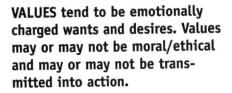

VALUES tend to be emotionally charged wants and desires. Values may or may not be moral/ethical and may or may not be transmitted into action.

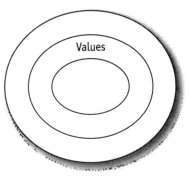

Values

Values are personal choices, relative to our own individual thoughts and feelings. It is important to understand that personal values are not always ethical. They may be right for a person, in a discrete moment in time, but not necessarily right and just for all people involved in the program. When a group of people, a team, an organization, or a league holds similar values in sport participation, there is a common morality. These are norms set by a group of people: parents, athletes, program directors, coaches, and the community. However, having a moral consensus does not necessarily mean that these shared values are right and just. Sometimes, the moral consensus favors elitism and "must win" values at the expense of player's enjoyment and satisfaction. Russell Gough, a sport philosopher, once said, "You can play by all the rules, and still be unethical."

Core Virtues On and Off the Field

Core virtues are considered universally desirable habits to which we hope all the people involved in the athletic program will aspire. These core virtues consist of, but are not limited to, the formation of a person's character through the learning of such traits as respect, responsibility, integrity (consistency of action), justice (fair play and respect for others), courage (founded in self-discipline, patience and perseverance), moderation/balance, and care and compassion. The healthy formation of an athlete's character, like the acquisition of a sport skill, requires hard work, consistent and faithful practice, patience, perseverance, and constant striving for improvement, along with respect for the advice of coaches, knowledgeable parents, and peers. Coaches, parents, and program directors strongly influence character development through the ideals and actions they present. Instilling a sense of right knowledge and action requires thoughtful reflection; only then will it produce consistent behavior and provide guidelines that help individual athletes aspire to right action.

VIRTUES are commonly accepted positive traits that transcend most creeds, cultures and communities. They are habits of the mind, heart and action and are always moral/ethical.

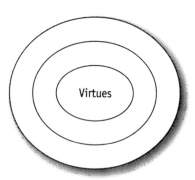

Views, Values, and Virtues in Action

The following pages illustrate differences among views, values, and virtues. As you study the scenarios and the responses from the adult mentors, note the differences in perspective, especially the differences in the virtues perspectives as compared with views and values. The box on page 33 provides further clarification of these differences. The importance of thoughtful reflection and the use of virtues as a foundation emerges clearly.

The point is this: If you declare that you run a character-based program, and your actions are based on views and values without regard to virtue, then your means and your ends are not in synch. This should send up a red flag. You need to make sure that the core virtues of the program are known, valued, and acted upon consistently.

Scenario One

A secondary school boy's hockey tournament game breaks out into a melee after the final whistle. The incident is spurred on by a frustrated player on the losing team who takes a swing at an opposing player. Before too long, more people are involved. Several players on the winning team are very active in the fight. According to State Association rules, the players involved are to be disciplined, including suspensions of several players from the winning team. They will not be able to play in the next game. However, their situation is brought to court and the players are reinstated—allowing them to play in the next state tournament game.

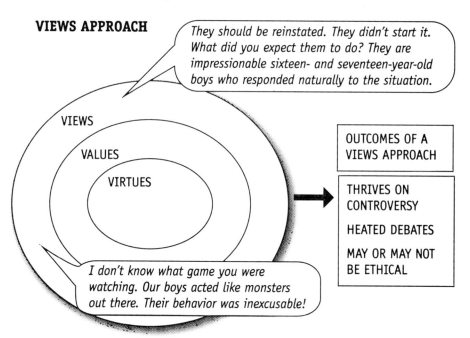

VIEWS APPROACH

They should be reinstated. They didn't start it. What did you expect them to do? They are impressionable sixteen- and seventeen-year-old boys who responded naturally to the situation.

VIEWS

VALUES

VIRTUES

I don't know what game you were watching. Our boys acted like monsters out there. Their behavior was inexcusable!

OUTCOMES OF A
VIEWS APPROACH

THRIVES ON
CONTROVERSY

HEATED DEBATES

MAY OR MAY NOT
BE ETHICAL

One coach suggests that "boys will be boys." The other coach claims that it doesn't matter who started the fight, all are guilty. He also called the players "monsters!" It's a good bet that this conversation will probably not be resolved based on the stances of the two coaches.

VALUES APPROACH

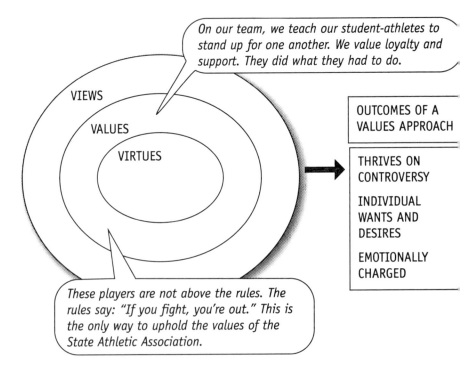

On our team, we teach our student-athletes to stand up for one another. We value loyalty and support. They did what they had to do.

VIEWS

VALUES

VIRTUES

OUTCOMES OF A VALUES APPROACH

THRIVES ON CONTROVERSY

INDIVIDUAL WANTS AND DESIRES

EMOTIONALLY CHARGED

These players are not above the rules. The rules say: "If you fight, you're out." This is the only way to uphold the values of the State Athletic Association.

One adult mentor declares that loyalty and dedication are important team values. However, the players backed up each other by fighting the other players. In this highly charged situation, there was little positive regard for the safety of all the participants involved. This type of loyalty and dedication is misguided. The values being used are clearly personal values, not necessarily a consensus of the core virtues of the athletic program or State Athletic Association. A values approach to sport takes on what people individually prefer. This tends to bring up strong opinion, backed by high emotion. The other coach stresses the importance of following the rules as a way to uphold the values that the State Athletic Association aspires to.

VIRTUES APPROACH

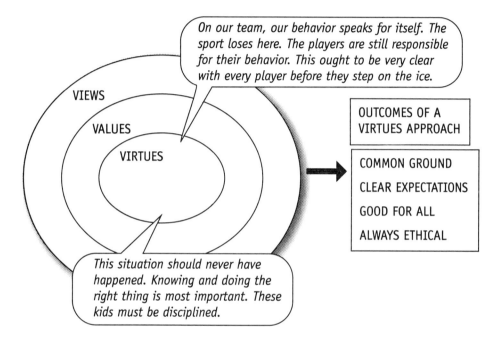

On our team, our behavior speaks for itself. The sport loses here. The players are still responsible for their behavior. This ought to be very clear with every player before they step on the ice.

VIEWS

VALUES

VIRTUES

OUTCOMES OF A VIRTUES APPROACH

COMMON GROUND

CLEAR EXPECTATIONS

GOOD FOR ALL

ALWAYS ETHICAL

This situation should never have happened. Knowing and doing the right thing is most important. These kids must be disciplined.

If a program's core virtues include respect for self and others, then it is the responsibility of the coaches to be very clear with their players about what respect ought to look like on the ice. When there is common ground on this issue, expectations and consequences are very clear. This ought to decrease the likelihood of problems.

Scenario Two

As a member of her town's ten and under soccer team, a nine-year-old girl is not seeing much playing time. At first, this didn't concern her. However, she is now becoming more disengaged from the process and not sure if she wants to stay with the team.

VIEWS APPROACH

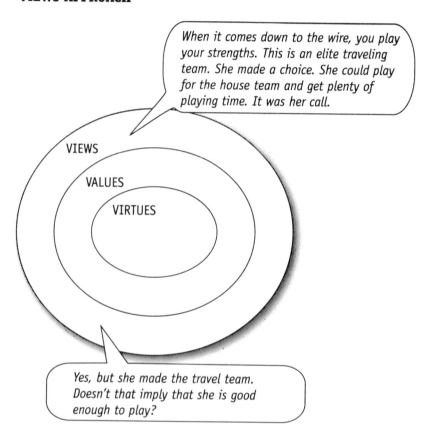

When it comes down to the wire, you play your strengths. This is an elite traveling team. She made a choice. She could play for the house team and get plenty of playing time. It was her call.

VIEWS

VALUES

VIRTUES

Yes, but she made the travel team. Doesn't that imply that she is good enough to play?

The first coach believes that the travel team ought to play the most talented players. The other coach takes issue and claims that a girl who is good enough to make the team should be allowed to play. These points of view can become heated and may not be resolved in a way that benefits the player and the program, in general.

VALUES

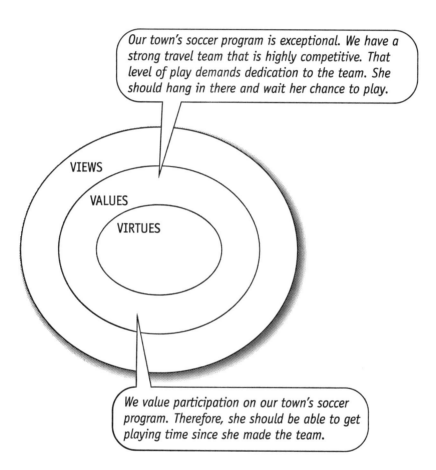

Our town's soccer program is exceptional. We have a strong travel team that is highly competitive. That level of play demands dedication to the team. She should hang in there and wait her chance to play.

VIEWS

VALUES

VIRTUES

We value participation on our town's soccer program. Therefore, she should be able to get playing time since she made the team.

The first coach declares that perseverance and dedication are important, regardless of playing time. The second coach claims that involvement—having the opportunity to play—is an important value of the town's soccer program. Dedication and participation, respectively, are important to each coach. Their individual preferences ought to be tested for consistency with the soccer program's stated mission.

VIRTUES

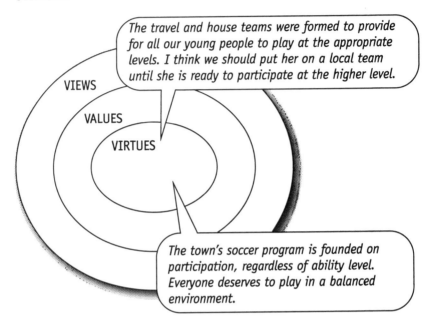

The travel and house teams were formed to provide for all our young people to play at the appropriate levels. I think we should put her on a local team until she is ready to participate at the higher level.

VIEWS

VALUES

VIRTUES

The town's soccer program is founded on participation, regardless of ability level. Everyone deserves to play in a balanced environment.

If a core virtue of the program is to value participation, then there is a responsibility of the adult mentors of the organization to make appropriate opportunities for involvement available for this girl. In the virtues approach, the foundation to the discussion is based on virtuous behavior.

Developing Virtue—The Forming of Character

One of the goals of this book is to provide information and instruction to coaches, athletic directors, and parents on ways to better teach proper behavior on and off the field. Character formation is not merely the development of skills, similar to dribbling a basketball or kicking a soccer ball; it is the acquisition of an enduring disposition, a way of living on and off the field—of knowing, valuing, and acting properly.

A person of good character possesses knowledge and attitudes that are consistent with behavior, and this benefits the individual as well as others. When properly developed, good

CLARIFYING THE DIFFERENCES		
Views	**Values**	**Virtues**
Thrives on controversy	Individualized standards	Universal standards
Heated debates	Emotionally charged	Common ground
May or may not be moral/ethical	May or may not be moral/ethical	Always ethical

character habits become automatic. We don't think about doing them; we just do them as a matter of second nature. We act in a right manner, because (1) it is the right thing to do, and (2) we have deliberately practiced this action as the right thing to do. The right action is founded in healthy contemplation and in the intention of doing what one would want others to do in those same circumstances—the Golden Rule.

Most people know the difference between the right and the wrong actions. However, it would be misguided to think that those who know and value what is right, always act on it. There are those who may not have been sufficiently exposed to goodness in their lives and, therefore, have difficulty acting in a right manner. Our hope is that the majority of young people's caregivers and mentors have acted in a right manner; and those with difficulties strive to follow the core virtues of the athletic program—at least for the sake of the athlete.

Misguided mentoring can be dangerous, since young people can model negative coaching behavior. Some coaches' vision of right action does not carry any farther than the tips of their noses, so they are unable to see the influence of their behavior on others. They may have the best intentions, based on what they know, and still act in a limited framework. Consequently, they act with a degree of selfishness. Coaches can get caught up in the expectations that end up driving their actions. Whether it be "ratcheting up" a program to a more competitive level or the desire to be coach of the year, the immediate gratification of the short term can take its toll on the coach and players in the long term. However, these coaches still have an obligation to help their student athletes aspire to being respectful and responsible on the field.

Developing good character habits requires time and experience. Becoming a "good sport" is a learned behavior. Being truly respectful to opponents and playing by the rules are dispositions that are developed over time and experienced on and off the field of play. "Sportsmanship" cannot be effectively taught and appropriately acted upon by merely saying it is "good." It must be reinforced through ritual and practice. There are far too many well-meaning parents, coaches, and program directors who believe that merely mentioning the words, "fair play" and advising a player to "be a good sport" will either reinforce or cause a change in an athlete's behavior. People ought to reflect and make conscious decisions to act consistently on these core virtues. This is the process by which we form excellent character habits. We must be aware that we are human and imperfect beings and sometimes the best we can do is to strive to attain this measure of moral excellence. A young athlete's intention to act well is highly influenced by the character habits he or she has already begun to acquire. By daily practice and ritual, the person reinforces the importance of making appropriate changes and calls upon the virtues to support such action.

States of Character

Whether it is a player, coach, parent, or official who has a weak or well-formed character, each brings his or her disposition to the playing field. Seldom can one "fake" who he or she is for an extended period of time. Some "moral lepers" can behave within the parameters of the rules, but the intensity of the sport experience tends to disarm the "weak of will" and expose people's personalities. This once again begs the question: Does sport build or merely reveal character?

Aristotle was helpful in distinguishing six states of character in humans. These states can be witnessed just as easily on the

FIGURE 2.1 Aristotle's Six Moral States: *Nichomachean Ethics* VII.1
and The Hard, Harder and Hardest Roads to Virtue
—Steven S. Tigner—

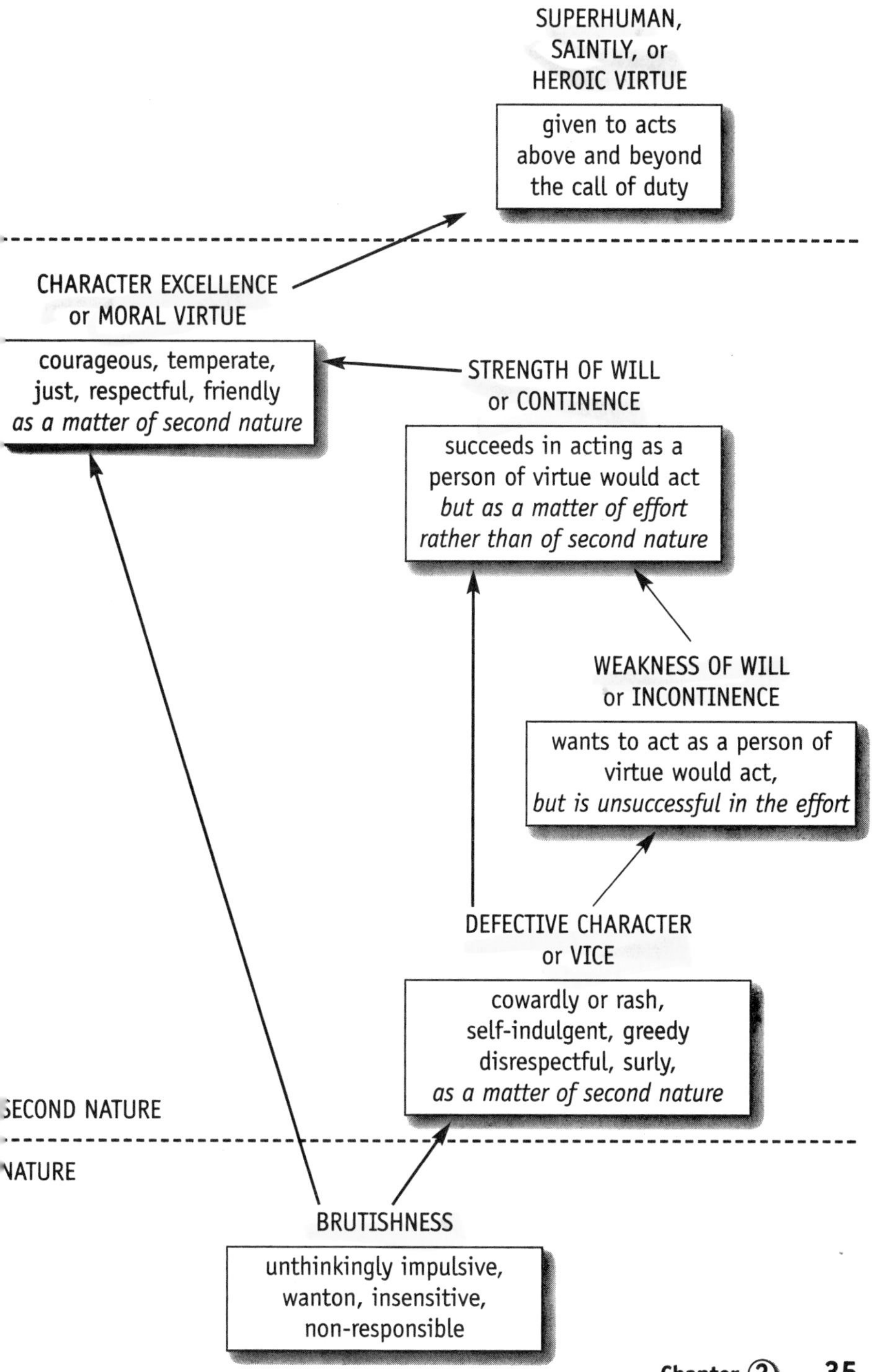

SUPERHUMAN,
SAINTLY, or
HEROIC VIRTUE

given to acts
above and beyond
the call of duty

CHARACTER EXCELLENCE
or MORAL VIRTUE

courageous, temperate,
just, respectful, friendly
as a matter of second nature

STRENGTH OF WILL
or CONTINENCE

succeeds in acting as a
person of virtue would act
*but as a matter of effort
rather than of second nature*

WEAKNESS OF WILL
or INCONTINENCE

wants to act as a person of
virtue would act,
but is unsuccessful in the effort

DEFECTIVE CHARACTER
or VICE

cowardly or rash,
self-indulgent, greedy
disrespectful, surly,
as a matter of second nature

SECOND NATURE

NATURE

BRUTISHNESS

unthinkingly impulsive,
wanton, insensitive,
non-responsible

playing field as any other place. Steven Tigner illustrates these states as (1) acting brutishly, (2) behaving self-indulgently, (3) aspiring to act with good character, but caving into temptation, (4) working to master temptation, (5) building self-discipline through reflection and moderation, and finally (6) acting with heroic excellence. It is important to know that this is not necessarily a stage process. Human beings have faults and imperfections and an act of moderation can change to one of self-indulgence at another given time.

All aspiring coaches, parents, and athletes are born **brutish** in nature. As infants, we were subjects of our own little world—crying for food and attention. Although most people advance from this primal stage, there are young people and adults who continue to act at the lowest form of character and do so without concern for others. Their behavior borders on the primal and animalistic, and is typically examined in actions of excessive output of selfishness. That's how infants, not adults, are expected to act. Brutish actions are upsetting and frustrating to most people. However, some sport participants unfortunately display a semblance of this behavior.

Because of the eventual consequences of acting brutishly, most people learn that this behavior is not acceptable in sport and in other aspects of life. Therefore, most young people and adults move up the "food chain" and eventually develop a sense of **self-indulgence**, a trait that is more common in young people and occasionally seen in adults. Those who act self-indulgently yield to their desires and are excessive and self-gratifying—as seen in their showboating or whining. Coaches do this when they have no hope of controlling their own sideline behavior. Athletes, who are obligatory exercisers, are self-indulgent when they tend to over-train without realizing the ramifications of their behavior on overall individual and team performance. Parents yield to their desires when they become so absorbed in watching their child play that their behavior disrupts the process of the game.

Fortunately, self-indulgent people who have come to realize that this action doesn't serve the good of others are capable of taking a large step in the development of their character. However, they may still be weak of will and **cave in to temptation.** People, who still can't seem to change their behavior, may know intellectually what they should do and how they should respond. They have the best intentions, but are lured into behavior that is self-serving. The athlete knows that he or she shouldn't say anything to the referee, even if it were a controversial call, but still does and is given a penalty, only to regret his or her action later.

However, through this struggle one may find the urge to persist, endure, and eventually reject the allure of the temptation, whether it be taunting a player, acting with intent to injure another player, or not practicing diligently to reach one's full potential. After struggling with temptation, a person's will may become stronger. Although he or she may still have a desire to act in a certain way, one is no longer controlled by it and will **master temptation.** A person will not act in a certain way, because through experience the behavior is known to be ultimately hurtful to self and others. Although, the impulse to act this way may still be present; the person chooses to act differently, and is, therefore, in control.

A virtuous state of character such as **moderation** is acquired through diligent ritual and rehearsal until the athlete or coach eventually is not tempted as often. Moderation differs from mastering temptation in that it is built on judgment derived from reflected experiences and artful narratives; it is balanced through precise thought about short and long-term consequences and clear goals, aspirations, hopes, and dreams. This person knows and performs right actions as a matter of habit.

The highest possible character state may be called **heroic excellence.** This highest state of character is displayed in acts of great courage or self-sacrifice that lie above and beyond the call of duty. These acts occur out of complete selflessness when people put themselves on the line without regard for their own benefit. We know of one high school athletic director who was willing to put his job on the line when he asked the school committee for the dismissal of a very popular, highly-connected coach who had witnessed and condoned an off-field self-indulgent activity by his team.

It would be absurd to think that one of the responsibilities of coaches is to move athletes through the states of character. Parents are the primary moral educators of their children and one of the parent's tasks is to assist his or her offspring as they eventually master temptation and develop a sense of moderation. This is the process of the formation of a child's will. Our hope is that the daily experience of our modeling appropriate behavior, carrying on simple, yet meaningful dialogue, and having logical consequences for inappropriate behavior on and off the field will help shape their character. However, as human beings, we are all fallible. Parents didn't go to school to become parents. They learned from their parents and others. Most do the best they can and hope that what they do is "good enough" to assist their child in forming a good character. Children go through stages of character formation that include caving into temptation (weakness of will); mastering temptation (strength of will); and for some, achieving a state of moderation or balance—knowing the right amount of action. Coaches are no different. Most have not studied to be coaches. They repeat the experiences, or sins, of the past. Some were privileged to have coaches who were good models and taught and practiced right action. So, when coaches, parents, and athletes arrive at the sport's venue, they bring their character development with them.

The Stupid Point

When people have developed a strong character, they have formed enduring habits of the head, heart, and hand. They know what is right and have continually practiced right action. So when an ethical dilemma arises, a coach or athlete with a well-formed character has less difficulty in making the proper behavior choice. Knowing, valuing, and acting on the good prevents the situation from becoming a problem. However, there are moments when coaches, parents, or athletes have known and valued the good, but have acted in a very different way. Ken Dryden, a lawyer and youth education advocate and formerly an outstanding professional hockey goaltender, claims that every person has a "stupid point." It basically means that most coaches, parents, and athletes know better, but the heat of the moment causes them to break down and act as if they had never been exposed to the "good" in their lives. We all make mistakes; however, a well-formed character helps limit these sojourns to the dark side.

In 1996, Dryden was asked to conduct an inquiry into a disturbing incident that happened in a Canadian college hockey game between the University of Moncton and the University of Prince Edward Island. Although the game itself had little media coverage, the local video tape of the event made its way throughout Canada and the United States. A controversial goal by Prince Edward Island's team prompted the Moncton goalie to rush immediately to the referee's side. As he put his arm on the referee's shoulder, other Moncton and PEI players joined the fray until the referee and goalie were surrounded. Suddenly, there was pushing, shoving, and punching. Dryden was asked to make sense out of this brief, yet highly disturbing event. Questions mounted, "How could such a thing happen."

"And the temperature rises," Dryden explained, "the distance between out of control *good,* and out of control *bad* is tiny. Our own personal 'stupid point' is always perilously near. Something happens, and we trip over the edge." However, a well-formed character decreases the odds of a person acting in such a brutish way. For example, we spoke with one high school assistant football coach who regularly had to restrain the team's head coach—a person who tended to "lose it" by the third quarter of the game. Although the head coach was consistent in reaching the stupid point, the players on the field and those on the bench had to witness behavior that is inconsistent with how coaches ought to act. This mixed message can cause confusion. Athletes know they would never get away with behavior like that.

Some athletes, parents, and coaches occasionally dismiss inappropriate adult or adolescent behavior in the manner that many people used to gloss over the behavior of a drunken person, saying, for example, that the intoxicated person has "had a tough run of luck." The equivalent to this on a playing field is to say something like, "Oh, they got caught up in the moment; the fever pitch of the contest brought them there. They normally don't act this way." The social and legal consequences for drunken behavior have dramatically changed in the past ten years. We are starting to see the same for problematic behavior at sporting events.

Establishing A Common Moral Language

It is essential that programs that say they are grounded in virtue have a common language. This language includes a simple understanding of what the character habits mean—how they are known, valued, and acted upon by parent, coach, and athlete.

Jeff Beedy, the headmaster at the New Hampton School and director of the character-based Sports PLUS program, suggests that coaches, athletic program directors, and parents can best communicate and educate through a common language, one that supports their philosophy. He says, "You don't need to display all the values (virtues). It's better to keep it simple. In a pluralistic society, many people may not relate to what these values mean." Several core virtues can be neatly defined so that all people involved in the athletic program can understand what each specific character habit means to them and to the success of the program.

FOUR CORE TRAITS OF SUCCESSFUL COACHES

Purpose—Vision
Goals, objectives, philosophy, and underlying principles establish the guidelines of the sports program

Skills—Competence
Proficiency in terms of the knowledge regarding sport
Ability to teach necessary skills
Effectiveness in communicating the priorities, goals, objectives, and culture
  of the program
Organizational skills

Relationship
Genuine caring about athletes
Respecting players
Concern for players
Knowing and understanding players
Ability to motivate

Character Habits
Solid work ethic
Exhibits responsibility, honesty, integrity, and dedication
Foster virtue in athletes

Boyea, 1994

The line can be applied to coaches. "Do you feel lucky?" Do you think you can be successful in your career if you don't have a clear sense of purpose; are not competent in the transfer of skills; do not genuinely care for the athletes; and have a reputation as a moral leper?

If you are not an upstanding citizen or lack the relational and character pieces, do you really think that you are that technically sound that you want to take the chance? You can get by —but for how long? This category of coach is extremely rare. Unfortunately, far too many coaches think their other abilities make it okay to cut corners. Some coaches just don't care about the relational and character dimensions.

Boyea's research suggests that coaches who are purposeful, skillful, relational, and have a well-formed character are able to create a success culture and sustain a "performance-conducive environment." Boyea's compelling findings parallel Denny Wright's examination of significant traits found in "superior" college coaches. Both assert that winning and character formation are not mutually exclusive. A superior coach's character doesn't change if the team wins or loses, performs poorly or performs well. The character traits most essential for the foundation of success are as follow: (1) honesty and fairness, (2) passion as the basis for quality, (3) concern for athletes, (4) competition as a cauldron of excellence, (5) quality instruction, (6) a balance between the present and future, (7) control of identity and ego, (8) time for praise and time for criticism, (9) resiliency in managing the peaks and valleys, and (10) the coach's responsibility for success and failure. Wright expresses each of these traits as a sentence statement, as shown in the box, below.

Wright and Boyea's research on coaching supports the earlier works of John Dewey. This process needs to be truly athlete-centered so as to allow the coach the opportunity to help the athlete develop skills into habits.

CHARACTER TRAITS OF THE SUPERIOR COACH

1. Honesty and fairness are the foundation for success.
2. Passion is the basis for quality.
3. Concern for athletes is essential.
4. Competition creates a cauldron of excellence.
5. Quality instruction brings success.
6. A balance between the present and future must be maintained.
7. Identity and ego must be controlled.
8. There must be a time for praise and a time for criticism.
9. Resiliency in managing the peaks and valleys is essential.
10. The coach must take responsibility for success and failure.

Wright, 1998

Teaching Skills and Habits

Teaching skill drills or character habits to athletes at the youth, secondary school, or college levels ought to be a well-thought-out process. Although skills and habits have some similarity, it is vital to understand the distinction between the two.

A skill is defined as a physical activity that is an "end in and of itself." To further clarify, a skill can be defined as an action that is "physically controlled" but not "socially directed." John Dewey offers a helpful illustration: "Suppose that conditions were so arranged that one person automatically caught a ball and then threw it to another person who caught and automatically returned it, and that each so acted without knowing where the ball came from or went to. Clearly, such action would be without point or meaning. It might be physically controlled, but it would not be socially directed." An activity that is not socially directed is one performed in relative isolation. An alternate definition of a skill, therefore, might be "know-how." It is an activity that can be truly mastered such as reciting the alphabet, brushing your teeth, or kicking a soccer ball.

A character habit, on the other hand, is defined as an action that is "socially directed." Character traits are developed by improving skills through deliberate practice until they become habitual—they become engraved. A person becomes disposed to acting in a certain way, because he or she has repeated the action over and over. You can imagine a character habit as an "internalized" skill—a disposition, or frame of mind.

Obviously, the teaching of skills is important. Skills become the foundation for character habits. Good coaches want their athletes to be more than robots, so it is important for athletes to develop habits from their skill work. Good coaches want their athletes to be passionate, creative, and empowered. Skills are "ends in and of themselves." Habit allows the athlete to venture beyond the world of skills to the world of meaning and purpose —to the ultimate goal of education and sports.

By reflecting carefully and closely examining the design of practice sessions, coaches are more inclined to create and sustain a blend of mastery and performance conducive to environments where habits are learned from skills. When athletes have a clear sense of purpose in a sport activity, they become "partners" in the process, rather than subjects under a coach's command. The meaning behind the skill promotes the acquisition of a habit. Habits cannot be learned in the same way a child learns the alphabet. It requires the relationship between pupil and teacher, or coach and player. It is only through relationships that creativity, passion, and empowerment can be conveyed.

Internalizing Virtue—Rehearsal and Reflection

Just as coaches support athletes in the process of acquiring and reinforcing technical skills and habits on the playing field, they have a unique opportunity to strengthen and support good character habits. The Internalizing Virtue Model (see Figure 3.1), developed by Kevin Ryan, Karen Bohlin, and Deborah Farmer, is a process that includes awareness, understanding, action, reflection, and the eventual acquisition of the virtue. They state that "internalizing virtue isn't just about acquiring a set of habits. It's about gradually gaining wisdom—acting and then reflecting on what we've done, learning from our mistakes, and coming to a greater understanding of how to live compassion, respect, or honesty."

The Progression for Internalizing Virtue

Awareness

First, coaches ought to explain and define virtues to their athletes so as to develop a common language that supports the shared mission of the athletic program. Athletes become **aware** that virtues such as respect, responsibility, and integrity are important parts of the whole sport experience. Awareness helps us all know the good.

Figure 3.1 Internalizing Virtue: An Instructional and Schoolwide Framework

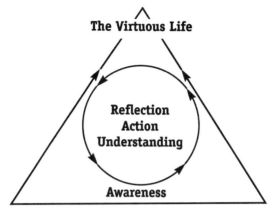

The Virtuous Life

Reflection
Action
Understanding

Awareness

Internalizing virtue isn't just about acquiring a set of habits. It's about gradually gaining wisdom—acting and then reflecting on what we've done, learning from our mistakes, and coming to a greater understanding of how to live a worthwhile life.

Why the circle inside the triangle?

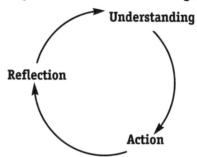

Understanding

Reflection

Action

- Our <u>understanding</u> informs our *actions,* our <u>actions</u> give us cause to *reflect,* and these <u>reflections</u> strengthen our *understanding* of virtue and our commitment to *act* accordingly.

Ryan, Bohlin, and Farmer, 1998

Understanding

Second, coaches can help athletes to develop an **understanding** of a virtue—what it looks like and feels like when it is lived. Understanding is enhanced through stories, images, and examples of sport past and present. Understanding helps us to value the good in that it allows athletes to contemplate the importance influence of virtue on enjoyment and performance.

An inspired coach's use of timely narratives can be quite riveting and can serve as an effective way to reinforce the influence of sport on character. From personal experience to the classics to current literature, the stories of an athlete's joys and frustrations on the playing field are brought to life by good coaches. When coaches tell stories, not just for entertainment, student-athletes are invited to journey into the deeper, more meaningful structure through which the purpose of the story is made clear. Stories that captivate players on a team can only be effective when they illustrate and instruct the athletes with information that makes sense and inspires wise actions. To tell a story of courage or respect is to possess someone in a way that reading a practice plan does not, and there is a natural human desire to be possessed in that way on occasion. Learning how to make up, tell, relate, and listen to a story of character is about balance and judgment. Children, adolescents, and even adults consistently respond to such illustrations.

Action

Although preparation is an important component of the sport experience, taking **action** on the playing field can also provide an enduring and compelling education. When we act on a virtue, we learn by doing. It is about doing the good. When we coach on the field, we declare to others what is important to us.

Reflection

Reflection is a thoughtful examination of our actions on and off the playing field. Were my actions appropriate? Did I make a wise decision or not? How might I do it differently at another time? Should I have yelled at the official? Did I do the right thing in not making the substitutions of players? Reflection is about knowing the good.

Virtue

People acquire a **virtue** when they have developed the ability to choose and act well. This happens when coaches, parents, and athletes consistently evaluate their actions through thoughtful reflection.

Cultivating Character Formation through Mentoring, Modeling, and Managing

The formation of character doesn't happen in a vacuum. It more often than not appears when good coaches take the risk to be fully present in their work with athletes. This means creating a genuine relationship between coaches and athletes—forged by healthy modeling, open communication, and logical expectations of behavior.

Coaches can be a significant influence in a student-athlete's moral and psychological journey from childhood to adulthood—a process that does not always happen without incident. Robert Kegan, a professor at Harvard University's Graduate School of Education, points out that we are asking a great deal of a young person—who, by definition, is struggling with observations and emotions about self and others—to see him or herself in a context that helps make sense of the world.

Not all young people implode under the stress of their social and familial odysseys. However, even for the most "competent," the most "self-efficacious," and the most "engaged," sorting out identity and relationship questions in isolation feels difficult. Some are fortunate to have enlightened parental support, but even they need the assistance of other caring adults, such as coaches, who will model positive behavior and act as mentors for them. However, if the objective is not merely to survive the journey but to prevail, to enter adulthood as a responsible, balanced person with the capacity to care for yourself and others, then the importance of positive and consistent mentors, models and managers cannot be overstated.

Mentoring

Good coaches are mentors to many of their athletes. The consistency of the coach's actions and words speaks volumes to the care that is directed toward the athlete. Sam Osherson, a psychologist who specializes in mentor relationships, suggests that by "showing up and being there" for young people, mentoring is mutually beneficial to both the athlete and the coach. In fact, one college athlete was surprised to receive a letter from his former high school hockey coach. Near the end of the letter, the coach wrote, "I take pride in knowing I was and am a small part of your life." The athlete sat back and reflected on this declaration. "Wasn't he simply my coach? Or is coaching more than just teaching the skills and strategies of the game?" Coaches, through their sharing of experience and wisdom, may receive the chance for reflection on the reciprocal influences of the coach-athlete relationship.

Osherson claims there are many internal and external pressures on student-athletes to perform in a variety of environments. He says that developmental uncertainty is a normal part of life and that meeting young people with their conflict is important. By way of their experience, good coaches bring a "shared wavelength" to the conversation with the athlete. By meeting the athlete at this level, they truly live in the skin of the young person.

Mentoring done "right" allows an athlete to see the coach as being fully human, not some sacred icon to be revered or demon to be exorcised. As mentors, good coaches are more than that; in that their humanness is exposed to the athlete. However, aspiring to be a mentor doesn't confer any assurance that a coach will make the connection with the athlete. Seemingly unsuccessful attempts of making connections with "at risk" athletes can be frustrating. We don't always know if we actually get through to them or not. Coaches, through the fact that their humanness and experience is exposed to the athlete, become more than just mentors. They become more human and, therefore, more attainable.

Carol Hotchkiss, the assistant head of school at St. Mary's Academy in North Carolina, claims that the "moment of connection" between a resistant young person and a caring adult may be acknowledged in a concealed manner without ever having a lengthy dialogue. As good coaches and mentors, we must trust the risks we take to open up the hearts of some of our challenging student-athletes. Our brief encounters with them cannot be evaluated in a win/loss column. All we can hope for is to have them realize their responsibilities and opportunities through the sport experience. In others words, we ought to support all athletes in attaining a sense of enjoyment and satisfaction as they strive to perform well on and off field.

Good coaches/mentors know that their athletes are more than centers and forwards—starters and substitutes. Knowing and calling a student-athlete by name means more than the greeting. It is a declaration of recognition of that person's presence—that he or she matters. As a substitute teacher in a Boston area high school, Mark Harris conducted an interesting exercise by learning the names of the majority of the student population. He claims that

> to remember names it is not enough to associate them to faces; faces can blend in the mind, and mistakes can be made. With the face one has to recognize the body, the voice, the posture, the habits, the responses. A person is a system of being in the world, and a name is the tag we attach to that total system. It encompasses quite a lot, not just a face. When I think of "Mickey Phelan" or "Claire Darcy," I associate a hundred things with each of them. Remembering just a name and a face is very hard; remembering a constellation of details about a student, paradoxically, is much easier and makes remembering the name and face a piece of cake. The students whose names I have a hard time summoning up are the ones I don't know much about. The elements of

names, the "Mikes" and the "Caitlins" and the
"Murphies" and the "Mitchells," are not unique,
but they stand for and indicate persons who are
unique and uniquely valuable.

Modeling

Good coaches/mentors are also influential modelers of behavior. Through their ideals, words, and actions, coaches set examples by "leading by deed." That is why good coaching consists of teaching athletes a number of small chains of consistent skill sets that help the athletes produce a variety of complex motions. Athletes also observe the consistency of the coach—they are very alert to adult hypocrisy. Adolescents respond strongly to adults who are clear about their adult responsibilities and appear to have influence. To a coach who has a well-formed character, this isn't even an issue. These actions are so habituated, that to do otherwise would never enter into the picture. Coaches can take advantage of teachable moments by displaying behaviors in difficult situations they would like their players to imitate. The coach should ask him or herself, "If the athletes on my team are a mirror of my actions, what do I see in the reflection?" Robert Wuthnow, the author of *Acts of Compassion,* once mentioned that "a role is something that you can take a vacation from. But a responsibility is something that is bonded."

If part of the coaching mission is to treat our student-athletes as whole people, it is important they know that we are not only coaches. Jerry Larson, the headmaster at the Cheshire School, claims that "we ask our students to assume a variety of roles during the school year. Shouldn't we as good educators ask ourselves to do the same? Besides our coaching responsibilities, we are also classroom educators, businesspeople, parents, husbands and wives."

Erin Quinn, men's lacrosse coach at Middlebury College, has received numerous coaching awards and epitomizes the ideal of good mentoring and modeling. However, Erin never played lacrosse. After an outstanding football career at Middlebury, he spent a great deal of time learning the technical and tactical components of the game under the tutelage of then head coach Jim Grube. After serving as graduate assistant and assistant coach, he eventually became the head coach. Erin's ability to model the behavioral expectations of his team—by having a solid knowledge of the game and a well-formed character—attracts many aspiring student-athletes to this serene campus in the mountains of Vermont.

Managing

Good coaches see the big picture and keep the projector in focus as they manage a jigsaw puzzle of responsibilities in serving their athletes. The vision consists of doing the right things, the right work, the right behavior, and saying the right words—all the time. When coaches lose sight of the mission, it puts stress on the program. Good programs don't explode and become bad programs—instead they fray. Managing the process, which includes following the athletic program's mission, is no easy task. It requires consistent supervision and evaluation.

Bob Bigelow believes that managing young people is a key to their enjoyment and satisfaction. He believes that there ought to be equal playing time for youth sports programs. If you have ten baskets in a large gym, you can have five games going on, instead of two. He observes that zone defenses for ten-and-under basketball smack of misguided management. When children do not have the opportunity to express themselves on the court, because the perimeter defense is impenetrable, it serves no one well, except the ego of coaches who are trying to have a shutout. Bob realizes that this is no easy task, as he has learned through his own teaching at basketball clinics—especially teaching the pick and roll drill. Bob's story of his learning experience appears in the box, page 66.

TEACHING THE PICK AND ROLL DRILL

(Or, Learning to Roll with the Drill You Pick)

Towards the end of the basketball season, I came in one morning to conduct a youth basketball clinic. I had exhausted all the simpler topics in basketball—shooting, passing and dribbling. So that particular day, I decided to teach them something I thought they could understand—the "pick and roll."

For those of you who don't know basketball, suffice to say that the pick and roll is a two-person maneuver that helps one of the offensive players get a better shot at the basket. So, with all good intentions, I walked into the gym to do a pick and roll clinic. If you have ever been around one hundred eight- and nine-year-olds on Saturday morning at 8:30 AM, you know it can be quite frantic. So my first order of business was to settle them down. The second piece was to settle the parents down. There were about thirty of them on the sidelines. Then I began the actual clinic by taking four of the boys to demonstrate the pick and roll.

Two play offense, two play defense. Of course, all of them were up to my hips, being eight- and nine-year-olds. And then I began, very well intentioned, to do my wonderful strategic nuances on the pick and roll. The great thing about eight- and nine-year-old kids is that if you are boring them, they will let you know right away. Lack of guile, I supposed. Within three to five minutes of my wonderful pick and roll clinic the kids were getting quite restless. So, I made a very quick determination and realized I could do one of two things: I could continue brow-beating them with the pick and roll for the next three hours. And I wouldn't get anywhere. Or I could do the right thing: Quit.

I did the latter. I didn't necessarily quit. However, I quickly eased myself out of the clinic. You know what the boys did? As fast as possible, they went and ran and grabbed all the available basketballs and started throwing them at the baskets and each other—which is, of course, what they really wanted to do on a Saturday morning. I went home with my tail tucked between my legs, because I had done one, lousy clinic. When I arrived home and started to reflect on what had just happened, I said to myself: "Bob, how many clinics have you done like that in the last twenty years? And you didn't recognize that the kids didn't get anything out of it."

I know the adults would get it when I did the clinics. They would come over afterwards and say, "Bob, great job." I taught them something. Didn't teach the kids a thing. So, I began to think about all my failed clinics the last twenty years. Upon watching a commercial about a brand new insurance policy that could actually be understood by normal human beings, a bright light in my head went on. The metaphor being used showed a college mathematics professor teaching arcane equations of calculus to the students, who just sat there with a bored look on their faces. Well, the commercial's intention was to show that this is a way insurance policy used to be written. And then I realized that my pick and roll clinic was like teaching calculus to third or fourth graders.

—Bob Bigelow

The best coaches create an environment to enhance performance so that people in the organization can do their best work with the least amount of distraction. Good coaches create a daily set of conditions, an environment. Mark Boyea's claims that a "performance-conducive" environment is one in which distractions are minimized for the athletes, allowing them to direct an optimal degree of their physical, cognitive, and emotional resources to the task at hand. If an athlete is confident that a coach is (1) competent, i.e., he or she clearly knows and understands the goals and objectives of the program; (2) trustworthy; and (3) caring—regardless of the coaches' personality or style, it stands to reason that the athlete will be better able to concern him or herself with performance than if any of these elements is missing. In other words, if a player believes that the coach is credible and he or she matters to the coach, then his or her abilities will probably be maximized.

John Pirani, the head coach of the Winchester, MA, high school boy's lacrosse team and a faculty member in the school's special-education department, believes that coaching management is one of the keys to enjoyment and improved performance. The field is the coach's classroom and the same level of control needs to be established. He says that there are typically four adults on the field that are primarily responsible for proper behavior during a game: the opposing two coaches and the two referees. When questioned about concerns of parents "butting in," he claimed that parents aren't responsible for the contest. They are guests who have a wonderful opportunity to watch their children play.

He has also seen the darker side. So, he speaks to the parents collectively prior to each season. He says, "I want you to be comfortable. I want your child to be comfortable. There shouldn't be a compelling reason to directly interact with your child during the game, so you don't need to stand on my sideline. Just watch the game and talk about it with your son over dinner." There is a compelling reason to empower parents to do what is right for their children. As an aside, his teams have won the past two state championships. John didn't adjust his stance on coach and parent responsibilities for the past two seasons. His consistency of management has been crystal clear to his athletes and other stakeholders in the community for many years.

Avoiding Misguided Compassion—The Integrity of Coaching

Good coaches want the best for their athletes; however, they must not forget their responsibilities to remain true to their character. Coaches must resist the temptation toward misguided compassion. We must be honest with athletes regardless of the emotional outcome. This is not an easy task, and can only be faithfully carried out if we, as coaches, aspire to do the right actions and say the right things individually as well as collectively. This gives athletes a strong message that coaches are true to who they are and are truly caring and compassionate. Thereby we encourage and enable athletes to aspire to the same ideals as we do.

Coaches act with misguided compassion when they keep quiet their disapproval of an inappropriate behavior or fail to express concern for a student-athlete at risk. Steven Tigner would claim that good coaches "fight fire with water whenever that is possible, but they know that sometimes it must be fought with fire and are prepared to do so." In order to maintain the integrity of the profession and to be truly compassionate, we must stand up for what is right and be prepared to "fight fire with fire," regardless of student-athlete or parent response. It is very likely that most coaches, at one time or another, will be tempted to act with misguided compassion.

When student-athletes or parents blatantly disregard the established core virtues of the athletic program, and no action is taken, the program begins to fray. In fact, when there are no consequences for unsportsmanlike behavior or no penalties for an athlete who consistently misses practices without a valid reason, then we protect people from the consequences of their actions. We prevent change from happening and prolong a misguided process that will eventually result in neutralizing the core virtues of the athletic program.

Tom Campbell, a high school teacher, parent, and youth sport's coach was asked by his community's youth soccer program if he would agree to be the president of the association. They had expressed interest in Tom because since he was perceived to be levelheaded and to do what was best for the young athletes on his teams—he would be perfect for the job! However, soon after he agreed to serve, a number of self-interested and entitled parents lobbied or complained about the state of the program—and about Tom's philosophy. They wanted preferred status for their own children. Nonetheless, Tom stated that he would follow the directives of the program and would not change or make exceptions for some of these "power" people. He didn't back down. He was an educator/coach who would not bend the rules, who believed in logical consequences for specific actions, and who believed in developing rather than simply rewarding talent.

The Reflective Coach

Like teachers, coaches ought to understand what part of the profession satisfies their altruistic needs and what part fulfills egocentric needs. In other words, we have desires and aspirations. It's about self and it's about others. It is part of human nature to want to be looked upon favorably; however, it is wrong for a coach to need or expect feedback from athletes to enhance one's sense of "self-importance." It should never be necessary for a coach to need athletes to applaud or act in ways that satisfy his or her ego. Many coaches claim that they want to pass on their own experiences or reflect on their own experiences—to understand why they are doing what they are doing. Some compelling observations on this matter come from Dr. Charles E. Red Silvia, the Springfield College swimming coach for 38 years. He coached over 200 All-Americans, and ten of his swimmers won NCAA Division II Championships. The following statement speaks eloquently to the issue.

*I look upon my role as a coach basically as an educa-
tor. I don't believe that as a coach, I have ever fallen
into thinking that I should be trying to expand my
personal reputation. I'm thinking about lasting experiences for my swimmers. Since many of them don't
swim competitively after they leave college, they
should take away with them some life lessons that
will benefit them later on—like the capacity to act
properly under stress.*

Although good teachers aspire to create meaningful and
worthwhile environments for their athletes, they are, by human
nature, fallible, and imperfect beings. Coaches do get tired and do
not always stay the course. When this period of low energy
occurs, it is essential that the good coach persevere by being
"good enough" on and off the field until the spark is re-ignited.
However, the long-suffering coach who goes through every practice with a "woe is me" attitude is cause for concern. Such a
teacher always has too much to prepare for, too many athletes,
not enough time, and consequently sabotages the team by living
in a world of alibi. A caring education can not come from such a
place. Without being self-disciplined to "know when to go and
know when to slow," good coaches can also become slaves to
themselves and their unrealistic expectations. Therefore, it is
right for good coaches to reflect continually on the nature of
why they coach, whom they coach, what they coach, and how
they coach. From this process, appropriate and practical strategies can be drawn. This, in turn, benefits the student-athletes,
and the entire athletic program in general.

Section **2**

Assessment

Discovering the Joy of Sport Throughout the Life Span

Sometimes when I consider what tremendous conse-
quences come from little things . . . I am tempted to
think there are no little things.
                                                    —Bruce Barton

After attending a CSI conference, one private secondary school athletic
director said she realized that she had no idea of what motivated her
coaches to be involved in the sport or sports at the level they were coach-
ing at their school. It occurred to her, that she hadn't thought or
reflected carefully about it herself. It was apparent that she was in a
good position to rediscover her sense of purpose in sport. After time
thoughtfully reflecting on her desires and motives for her involvement in
sport, she then met with each of her coaches to ask them to declare
themselves also.

If someone were to ask you "what" you think and "how"
you feel about sport, you would respond naturally and fluidly.
You might explain your excitement or frustration with various
aspects of competition or your interest in the opportunities
sport participation present to young people. Your response
would reveal your attitudes and biases, spoken as though they
had been rehearsed daily.

Now, suppose a thoughtful friend or colleague were to frame the question differently and ask you not "how" you feel about sport, but "why" you feel as you do. This person would have asked you the "right" or more significant question. This is the question everyone involved in sport needs to have answered for him or herself.

Let's start with a simple exercise. Begin with another line of questioning. What sport experience is most memorable for you and why? Why do you participate in sports? What is the athletic memory you carry around with you that allows you to make sense of your views on sports or, in some cases, your sense of yourself? Was there a most important, defining, sport moment for you? Was it something that sustains you now, in a positive sense? Did it support your sense of identity? Or did it make you uncomfortable? Angry? Less than complete?

Each of us has a personal history with sport about which we must reflect if we are to make sense of our true thoughts and feelings and be clear about what we are passing on to the young people we work with on our teams or even in our own families. We are all products of our histories and environments, and we need to understand "why" as well as "how" and "what" our experiences have taught us.

Sport Participation Throughout the Life Span

In addition to our personal histories, we can observe the patterns of human development that can guide our reflections on these matters. The CSI has constructed a life-span sport-participation model that parallels other social development paradigms. The model speaks to the sport experiences of people throughout their lives, and how the childhood and adolescent experiences of adult coaches influence how they serve their student-athletes. The box, page 75, outlines the overall model; the following discussion takes a close look at each element.

> **LIFE-SPAN PARADIGM**
>
> Informal Structure
> Freedom of Movement
> Challenge/Exploration
>
> The Formal Structure
> Purity of Experience
> Contamination of
> Experience
> Integration of Experience

The Informal Structure

Generally, we first experience freedom of movement as infants. We are not restrained in our actions, and we are encouraged to respond instinctively to our surroundings. Some modern psychologists might suggest that the total freedom of a baby's movements produce a "flow" state, a concept associated with the extraordinary performances of elite athletes. "Flow," described simply, is the feeling of control and confidence one has when the challenge of the task is matched by the skill to handle that challenge. In the state of original freedom, the newborn moves naturally and easily.

Freedom precedes a second stage: challenge and exploration. As with freedom, the challenge is self-imposed at first and related to one's self-development. In this stage, crawling, sitting, moving intentionally through space, acting, or performing a task help infants develop an emerging sense of control over themselves and their physical space. In this stage the infant begins to explore and try new tasks and form an understanding of its capabilities, as well as its limitations. What is most important, however, is that the infant defines these qualities, not someone else who measures what is valuable or successful. The other value of this stage is the purity of the experience. Tasks are undertaken for the sheer joy or interest associated with them.

Following these initial stages is the introduction of a more structured means of controlling movement and enhancing opportunities for learning and growth. Parents and caregivers provide new tasks and challenges as they begin to influence and direct the exploration phase. Usually, this early structure retains the purity of the internally motivated play of the infant or toddler. Adults encourage skill-building and cognitive development through this direction. They also begin to introduce the earliest forms of athletic coaching as they help the child learn about throwing and catching, running, and climbing. With adult involvement, children begin to understand the concept of "right" and "wrong" ways to do things, as well as the idea of competition: higher, farther, faster. Although this competition is with self or only against a standard set by a caring other, a child's ego development is more directly in the process of being formed.

Obviously, children need direction and support as they develop. While the importance of free play as a learning experience should not be underestimated, most people understand that adults are in a better position to guide and organize activities for their children than are the children themselves. Still, adults need to understand their own attitudes about competition and sport so that they are clear about and careful with the messages they transmit to their offspring. Parents who have not had positive modeling in this aspect of development often pass on their negative attitudes without realizing it. In their enthusiasm to push their children to excellence too quickly, they run the risk of challenging the child beyond his or her skill level and may create frustration or discouragement.

This type of contamination is not as evident as one might expect; subtle indicators might be a child's negative reaction to failure or unwillingness to continue with an activity that is not producing the positive reinforcement the child has come to expect. Yes, structure is appropriate, but purity of structure is the goal. The formation of good habits results from thoughtful construction of structured challenge and support at this stage.

Formal Structure

Formal structure follows the informal experience as young people are introduced officially to competition. In some cases today, four-year-olds are participating in soccer leagues where coaches are motivated by their own needs to help children understand the complexities of winning and losing. Most parents have had to make difficult decisions in navigating the hazards of informal structure. There are precious few "How To" manuals dedicated to this subject of helping parents provide guided play. Imagine how much more is at stake when parents turn some of the responsibility for character and habit formation to someone outside the family.

Many parents may have successfully plumbed the depths of their own sport experience and discovered the hidden agenda there. Whether positive or negative, they have understood what motivates them as teachers and coaches and have fashioned an approach accordingly. Are they now prepared to hand this sacred responsibility of character formation over to an adult about whose history and motivation for involvement in sports they have no information?

This is a serious concern, given the horror stories they have heard about youth sports. Is this new challenge going to be educational and thus beneficial, or will it be detrimental for their child? Will their daughters or sons learn from a coach that winning is good and losing is bad? Will their children equate being successful in sports with being successful as a person? Will they be able to discriminate between having a problem with a skill and having value as a person? Will their children continue to experience the joy of movement and the exhilaration of sport, knowing that competition can also be pure and positive? It may all depend on the core virtues, or lack thereof, and experiences of the adult who will be the model and teacher for their children.

Integration

As young athletes move through their experiences within the formal structure of sport, they typically experience an awareness of or an awakening to the realities of involvement in sport. Some realize that things are not always fair. Others become aware that losing hurts, but is part of the experience. People discover the presence of greed, ego, passion, collaboration, fun, pain, fallibility, and limitations. Self-confidence is built or fractured.

This is the period where healthy and thoughtful adult guidance is imperative. Young people will make sense of this information and experience on their own, but the process is better directed by reflective adults who know right action, value it, and act on it. These adult mentors have integrated their earlier sport experiences into their teaching and coaching. Not everyone attains integration in the same way or at the same time, but all make their own sense of what sport participation means or has taught them. For many people, the majority of the experiences are pure in nature—sport is an enjoyable and satisfying venture. Unfortunately, for other young people, their youth sport experiences may be painful reminders that what is intended to be a joyful experience can eventually become contaminated. Adults who have had earlier negative experiences may not even be aware how they model those experiences in their coaching behaviors.

Since our own experiences and those of our children's coaches are so important in understanding "why" we think about sport and competition as we do, we need to find a way to access that information. We need a vehicle to assist us in this search. Coincidentally, a significant number of leading business and corporate entities have discovered the need for a similar tool to support their managers and executives. 3M, Westinghouse and PepsiCo have integrated various forms of introspection training with their management development programs.

These exercises emphasize the importance of self-reflection as a means to understanding oneself. If you understand yourself and what motivates you, you can be more effective in making plans for the future. A piece from the *Harvard Business Review* describes the new manager/coach who has "the opportunity to engage more thoughtfully and actively in reflection. Taking the time to reflect formally during these processes is the key to whether the process becomes a mechanism for change." If you don't know where you've been, you cannot understand where you are. If you don't know where you are, you have little chance to move forward positively.

Our response to the importance of thoughtful, directed, self-reflection is the Sport Experience Questionnaire (SEQ). This intentionally uncomplicated questionnaire (see Figure 4.1) comprises seven basic questions regarding one's own experience with informal and formal structures and the lessons of integration. This assessment tool focuses on memorable experiences with physical movement and sport and invites the participant to reflect on the lessons and meanings of those experiences. What people value most, the foundations of their character, is elicited from the responses. The use of narrative, even in abbreviated form, offers the opportunity to consider, or reconsider, the importance of one's perspective on early physical and athletic experiences. Coaches, parents, athletic directors, school administrators, even student/athletes, benefit from the chance to discover the interdependence of the lessons, experiences, and examples through which they have arrived at adulthood.

The Sport Experience Questionnaire

Our limited inquiry to date gathered data from two primary groups: (1) adult coaches and athletic administrators, and (2) middle and high school students. The results are predictable, yet especially noteworthy. Our adult respondents have been remarkably consistent in recalling their earliest experiences with physical movement. These memories parallel the "freedom" of movement and the "exploration/challenge" phases of human development. Rolling around on the living room rug, taking one's first steps, or escaping from, climbing beyond, or trying to keep up with the adults in one's life dominate the responses.

FIGURE 4.1. Sport Experience Questionnaire

The Sport Experience Questionnaire is designed to provide information about your participation in sports throughout your life. We thank you in advance for completing this anonymous form as fully as possible. You may answer the questions in a narrative (sentence) form or in short phrases (bullet-points).

Age _____ □ M □ F

Please check all that apply:

□ Current Athlete □ Teacher/Coach □ Parent □ Former Athlete

□ Official □ Youth Program Director

□ School Administrator: □ Elem. □ Secondary □ College

1. What is your most memorable sport experience (positive or negative)? At what age? Why?

_____

_____

_____

2. Why do you participate in sports?

_____

_____

_____

3. What do you remember about your first sport experience? At what age?

_____

_____

_____

4. Are there any aspects of your sport experience that have changed your perspective on sport in general? If so, what and when?

_____

_____

_____

5. What are your current personal reflections on your sport experiences?

_____

_____

_____

6. List and describe three values that you have derived from sport participation.

_____

_____

_____

7. Name three people who have had the greatest influence (positive or negative) on your sport participation. Why?

_____

_____

_____

Our adult respondents' earliest memories of a formal or informal sport experience provides a first clarification of the differences between "purity" and "contamination." Some recall the thrill of being in uniform; others remember being intimidated by the formality and competitiveness of the situation. Some recall supportive, caring grown-ups, while others envision overly demanding adults (parents and coaches) who spoiled the purity of the moment. A number of respondents report freedom and fun, but others describe failure, pressure, and self-doubt. On balance, first sport experiences are positive; but when they are not, participants seem to carry the consequences with them forever.

As reported in the SEQ, respondents' most memorable sport experiences generally depend on when the event occurred. There are, however, basic categories into which nearly all information falls: (1) The respondent produced the winning run, hit, basket, touchdown; (2) The team **I** played on won the championship; (3) The team **I** coached became a great team—won games and developed a positive identity. Often these experiences are similar to the Rocky Balboa type, victory with the odds stacked heavily against them.

Generally speaking, if the event occurred before age fifteen, the "I triumphed" theme applies. From fifteen to eighteen years of age, the success of *team*, commitment to *team*, and importance of *team* supercede and define personal success. Finally, responses chronicling coaching success seem to reinforce either early adolescent or late teen experiences, "I coached x team or individual to success" as opposed to "Our *team* triumphed over insurmountable odds to become a great team."

There are no real surprises here. Early adolescence is about identity formation, while late adolescence focuses more on fidelity and the dual concepts of competition and cooperation. Unfortunately, contamination experiences are reported, and they fall within the same parameters: "I was humiliated" or "The *team* was coached by a person who cared more about winning than about the well-being of the athletes in his/her care."

The personal reflection question elicits memories of the joy of sport, the friendships forged during competition—with teammates and with the opponent—and the hard work. When participants respond, they generally are looking back at their sport experiences with the perspective of many years. They reflect on the overall experience—"would not trade it" as opposed to "would not wish it on someone else." They explain the discovery of reality—"hard work pays off" and "effort does not always guarantee success." Some describe their commitment to pass along, or not to carry on, the positive or negative lessons learned on the fields, courts, mats, and tracks.

The most telling responses seem to be contained in the last two questions: "List and describe three values that you have derived from sport participation," and " Name three people who have had the greatest influence (positive or negative) on your sport participation." Why? Once again, the consistency of the answers suggests a clear pattern. Those with positive stories describe *teamwork, hard work,* and *respect* as the most important values learned. They were shown how to make a commitment to others, to work hard (develop a work ethic), and to respect others and themselves. They learned how to compete as well as how to cooperate. Seldom did the respondents mention "learning how to win" or the "receiving recognition" as values acquired from sport.

The responses about who influenced them and what the influence was are similarly uniform—Dad, coach, and then a sibling, a different coach, or a peer. Their lessons: the parent or coach "modeled good behavior" (provided a role model), "cared about me and had faith in me," and "taught us the value of hard work." Rarely did respondents mention "winning" as an important influence. When it was brought up, the comments were normally part of a tale of contamination, undue pressure, wrong-headed motivation, or insensitivity and selfishness.

The participating coaches and athletic administrators remember their adult coaches, many years later, as the people who helped them develop good character habits, who led by deed, and who expressed interest in them as people. As far as they were concerned, these were the hallmarks of great coaching. Fundamentals, knowledge of the game, toughness, and success may have been issues at some point in their lives, but these topics were not the objects of their thoughtful reflection; and we were not surprised. Actually, the responses of the students in our research turned out to be predictive of these results.

Adolescents, in general, do not have as much to share about their earliest memories of physical movement. Their answers remind us of the importance of social interaction in human development. Their remembrances are informed by their parents' stories of early walking patterns, rambunctious behavior or idyllic experiences with family. Their first sport experience is something they recall vividly, reminding the CSI investigators that the movement from early to late childhood and the introduction to "formal structure" is an important part of identity formation. Little League, peewee football and hockey, and youth soccer dominate their answers as they remember the thrill of victory and the agony of not measuring up. Contamination experiences, especially with overly aggressive parents (as coaches and fans) are prevalent in these accounts.

Their answers to the question of perspective are also germane. They have discovered that sports are serious, more like work than play. They realize for the first time that you can get hurt in formal athletics, and that sport participation can reveal as well as develop character. They wonder about emphasis, pressure, and winning and losing; and they articulate most definitely their observation that adults don't always act as adults should. They puzzle over the question of whether losing makes you a loser, whether it somehow compromises your worth. As they move toward identity formation (or identity confusion) and integration, they are working hard to clarify the messages and the rules of engagement.

Our primary focus, however, has been on their responses to the "three values" and "three influential people and their lessons," to determine if the life-span paradigm applies with younger athletes. Adolescence, according to most educational theorists and psychologists, presents unique challenges and opportunities to the young person going through it and to the adults working as guides or companions (parents, teachers, and coaches). Adolescents are developing physically (biologically), individually (personally), and socially (as citizens, team members, parts of the whole); and all three types of development need to be addressed in their sport experiences.

These young people are especially impressionable, because during these years (fourteen to eighteen) they depend on what Erik H. Erikson, the noted social psychologist, refers to as the "radius of significant others" for models of leadership and lessons in friendship, competition, and cooperation. Adolescents are looking to refine their capacity to care about and to trust others, and they enter this phase of their lives with an idealistic view of the world. They are, at once, experimenting with the competing needs for "isolation" and for "intimacy." They desperately need thoughtful adult guidance during this time, and they are more open to and appreciative of it than is generally assumed. Consequently, their answers to these questions provide important information for any adults involved in youth or high school sports, as coaches or parents.

Our student SEQ's are also remarkably consistent with those of coaches. The young athletes initially talk about learning the importance of "having fun," but quickly move to the other values learned: "persevering" and "being part of a team." Depending on their age, their opinions focus either on self (younger) or other (older). Comments about self include fun, self-efficacy, the primacy of care and concern, limitations, and the ability or inability to commit. Values focusing on others relate to team, respect for others (opponents) and fairness. Students rarely mention new skills or techniques. They discuss an adult's actions in terms of being consistent with or contradictory to the behavior they expect from any and all adults.

When adults do not show or express care and concern, when adults are not positive role models, or when they promote values or allow behaviors not consistent with an adolescent's ideal world view, the adolescents become confused or disappointed. Depending on the nature of an adult's behavior, young athletes may experience a helpful boost toward integration or an unfortunate shove into contamination. The adolescent participants move from seeing sports as "fun" when they are young, to being introduced to hard work in middle adolescence, and experiencing a job-like activity or a commitment that defines them as older athletes.

The research shows that the highest sport dropout rates occur among youngsters ages twelve and thirteen. This is no surprise.

Many younger athletes join sports activities for the fun and the social benefits. When the activity becomes more like a job, or when it feels like something that is more "about the adults" involved than "about the athletes," the young participants may decide it's not for them. Adults need to understand this aspect of adolescent development and support the young athlete's transition from self to other and from pure fun to enjoyable, structured experience.

The athletes' responses to role models and influential people differ slightly from those of the coach participants because our youngest respondents include professional athletes in their list of heroes. There are still three distinct categories of responses:

1. Younger athlete (thirteen to fourteen) include mostly parents and professional athletes;

2. In the middle years (fifteen to sixteen) they shift their attention to parents and coaches equally;

3. Older adolescents (seventeen to eighteen) refer almost exclusively to coaches.

The responses take us through the developmental stages outlined earlier. The transition is from focus on fun, support, and entertainment (category 1) to a focus on performance and perseverance (category 3).

The SEQ investigation is potentially compelling for two reasons. First, the information reinforces what we know about how young people develop and what they want and need from adults. Athletic programs are supposed to support our children and athletes in their effort to make sense of their worlds—to continue a healthy pattern of cognitive and social/emotional growth. Coaches and athletic administrators have the opportunity, as well as the responsibility, to ensure a safe, challenging, supportive, and developmentally appropriate experience for their athletes. The coaches are extensions of both the parents and the child's teachers as important educators.

All coaches need to remember that care and concern are primary values for the athletes. Coaches need to be aware that their actions speak more loudly than their words. They need also to understand the importance of being consistent and reasonable in their behavior and their expectations. The best coaches will, as Erikson suggests, "practice restraint, charity, and compassion." Restraint means to be "care-ful" with adolescents. Charity suggests the capacity to take "care of" young people. Compassion defines the desire to "care for" those in one's charge. These qualities characterize the thoughtful, responsible adult whom all parents would support as a role model for their children.

The following box refers to the values derived from sport and people who had the most influence on sport participants.

RESULTS OF THE SPORT EXPERIENCE QUESTIONNAIRE			
VALUES:			
Coaches	Athletes		
Teamwork	Teamwork		
Work Ethic	Fun		
Respect	Perseverance		
INFLUENTIAL PEOPLE		WHY INFLUENTIAL?	
Coaches	Athletes	Coaches	Athletes
Dad	Parents/Pros	Role Model	Role Model
Coach	Parents/Coach	Care/Concern	Care/Concern
Coach/Peer	Coach	Work ethic	Confidence

Second, the SEQ investigation validates our belief that thoughtful reflection provides an effective means for discovering one's motivation for and attitude toward sport. Self-reflection helped our participants remember where they had been, discover where they were, and begin to determine where they needed or wanted to go. These participants were surprised that both their athletes and they valued the same things. They were surprised to uncover, or remember, what they valued in their sport experience.

They were even more surprised to realize that they were not acting on what they valued, in all situations. They were shocked when their memory search provided them with clues and ideas about what they needed to do in the future to be the kind of coach they had experienced or longed for as young athletes. It was therapeutic for them to remember the significant names and lessons of the past. For some, the memorable moments had always been a part of their consciousness. For others, the important experience seemed almost surreal or dreamlike. They had never processed the situation fully, and they desperately needed to understand the experience. To appreciate how vivid and meaningful such memories can be, consider John Buxton's recollections of a wrestling match that occurred when he was in the eighth grade, as shown in the box, page 00.

We all have our personal stories, our favorite sports anecdotes. Rather than suggest that you express them in a narrative form, as we have in this chapter, we would encourage you to plumb the depths of your memory by asking probing questions. You need to discipline yourself to discover what your sport experiences meant to you. How did they shape you? What did they mean, individually and collectively, to and for you? What are your sports values? Do they reflect the important lessons you learned in sport? Are you aware of the influence you have on those you coach? Do you approach your sport with respect for it and its traditions? For your opponent? For your athletes? For yourself?

These self-reflection exercises are easier when you have spent more than two decades coaching and thinking about the sacred trust a coach inherits along with the whistle. When you are twenty-five, you are still close to the game, to the hard work, and to the competition. The impact you have on your athletes probably is more immediate than is that of a more experienced coach. Perspective, however, is more elusive when you are young, so the more time you spend reflecting on your experience, your opportunities, and your significant responsibility to help young

WRESTLING WITH THE GORILLA

I had an unforgettable experience which occurred in the eighth grade. I remember the details as if the match took place yesterday. And whenever I have been in a management workshop, a leadership or sports psychology class, or a serious conversation about sports or life with athletes or coaches, the specifics of the event rush back into my mind. I was thirteen, weighed ninety-nine pounds, and was wrestling for the Varsity in the 110-pound weight class. Our team was competing in a significant pre-season tournament, against a number of larger schools with far more accomplished programs. It was the end of the day and I was the only wrestler from our school still competing. My opponent in the match for third place was a Mighty Mouse look alike, as big as a Gorilla, with a five o'clock shadow. His muscles and his whiskers were enough to convince me that I didn't belong in this obvious mismatch.

I was somewhat skilled but seriously underpowered, so my strategy was to keep it close and not embarrass myself. Suddenly, it was the beginning of the third and final two-minute period, and I realized I was only losing by two points, 5-3. I engaged myself in debate. Lose by two and it's a moral victory. Don't get pinned; too much pride for that. Don't risk putting yourself in danger just to be a hero. Keep it close and everyone wins. However, just when I had convinced myself that discretion would be the better part of valor, something else entered my mind. Escape, take him down, and win. What have I got to lose? If I don't try, I lose anyway.

The referee blew his whistle, and I exploded in a frenzy of activity. Everything I had, every ounce of resolve and effort was focused on the goal. But my attempts were thwarted. Try, fail. Try again, fail. Time was running out. Thirty-five seconds left in the match. I would not be denied. With five seconds remaining, the referee slapped the mat. I had pinned the gorilla. I had tamed the wild beast. I had overcome my own fear and had been rewarded for the effort. As the referee raised my hand to signify the victory, I fainted. I must have emptied the tank, pushed myself to the point of exhaustion.

When anyone asks me if I have ever had a moment in sports that influenced my values or outlook on life, that match flows back to me immediately. It has taken on more importance for me than winning subsequent championships, playing three sports in college, or competing for national titles. Those two minutes taught me that I could influence the outcome of a contest or a situation. I would never be afraid to give my best effort, even if I was unsure of the outcome. I had a responsibility to myself, to my team, and to my opponent (metaphorically) to give my best effort.

That match has influenced my attitude in my work, my approach to raising a family, and my philosophy as a long-time coach. The opportunity to recall and reflect upon that event and that decision-making process proved to be extremely significant for me. Since the event took place when I was thirteen years old, my focus, predictably, was on the "I" aspect of the experience. A memorable moment later in my development would probably read quite differently. Nevertheless, the point is clear. We need to remember where we have been and understand where we are, before we decide where we should go and how we can get there. My story has served me well throughout my life span. My experience happened to be positive and sustaining, but had it been negative, it would still benefit me to reflect upon it, understand it, and learn from it.   — John Buxton people learn and develop, the more effective you will be as a mentor and an influential adult in their lives.

Robert Kegan in *The Evolving Self* describes how important outside influences are in the developmental process. His words provide a fitting conclusion to this chapter:

> *Who comes into a person's life may be the single greatest factor of influence to what that life becomes. Who comes into a person's life is in part a matter of luck, in part a matter of one's power to recruit others, but in large part a matter of other people's ability to be recruited. People have as varying capacities to be recruited as they do to recruit others. If the capacity to be recruited is educable and depends in part on our ability to see, then perhaps the kind of exploration we undertake in a book like this one [The Evolving Self] can enhance our recruitability. Accordingly, this book is concerned with practice as well as theory, with the responsibility of our response-ability, with the question of what we do once recruited.*

> *And yet however much we learn about the effort to be of help, we can never protect ourselves from the risks of caring, which separate real help from advice, reassurance, or consolation. In running these risks we preserve the connections between us. We enhance the life we share, or perhaps better put, we enhance the life that shares us.*

The primary aspect of participating in sports is not only to enjoy life, but also to become a part of it. The pinnacle of participation is just another facet of life in that we merge with life, becoming another part of it and enhancing it.

⑤

The Formal Structure
of Athletic Programs

Authority and accountability must be based on an institution's structure that serves the establishment of common purposes and the protection of liberty.
Edwin J. Delattre—*Education and the Public Trust*

In the movie Sandlot, a group of neighborhood boys gather at the local sandlot to play pick up baseball. They share stories and confront their own issues and demons in the context of their journey from childhood to adolescence. Their world does not include uniforms, coaches, parent fans, or even baselines. Their equipment is minimal, and their expectations are limited to improving skills and having fun. In this venue they learn from their experiences and from each other about life.

Many baby boomers viewed this film nostalgically as a window to the way it (sports and childhood experiences with sports) used to be or was meant to be. When they [we] were young, on days when there was no school—the days of vacations and summer—we spent our time in the company of friends, playing. Some boomers reacted with surprise that these youngsters were allowed to be away from home for the day without parent supervision or beepers.

Was there actually a time when kids were allowed to schedule their own days, work out their own problems, and grow up with relatively little social programming? Should we turn the clock back and eliminate all the professionalism that has crept into our children's games? Personally, we believe that children have too little opportunity to work things out and make decisions for themselves in today's world. Most young people need a "day planner" to keep their appointment schedule straight. Parents not only orchestrate the program for their kids; they participate in the activities to an extent never imagined even twenty years ago. Little-League practices attract larger parent audiences than games used to, and with the video equipment available, parents have the technology to bring all their Little Leaguers' accomplishments and mistakes back into the home for analysis and further commentary.

That said, the world of drive-by violence, neighborhood drug trafficking, and the plethora of crimes against the innocent has made many neighborhoods places where sandlot play cannot be a reality. Life has become too fraught with danger for our children. Nevertheless, there are aspects of the *Sandlot* experience that merit attention. Recall the role of the significant adult in the film. Kids at play often created legends and myths to explain away their fears. Sometimes, in spite of their best intentions, children need adult guidance and intervention in order to get things right, to put them in the proper context. The wise counsel of a caring adult can make all the difference in some critical situations. Our current reality necessitates adult involvement in the lives of our kids. Thus the creation of a formal structure for sport.

Historical Perspectives of the Formal Structure of Organized Sport

Discussions of organized sport hearken back to a time long before the 1950s, or even before the Norman Conquest of 1066. Twenty-two centuries ago, Plato held forth on the importance of both play and sport. He must have understood the opportunity represented by children's play. He concluded, after some deliberation, that unstructured play was a growth-filled experience for young people. However, the lessons that could be taught in structured play were so significant in the formation of the adult character, that for the good of the Republic, adults should guide young citizens' play to ensure that the right and just attitudes were cultivated. Plato obviously understood the intrinsic educating power of sport and, therefore, the necessity of having mentors and guides frame the experience for the participants. Plato saw the need for responsible, value-centered coaching, something we seek centuries later.

While there are legions of coaches who perform their duties well, there are too many who lead us to the conclusion that kids would be better served if adults left them to their own devices. No adult egos, arguments, control issues, or the need for vicarious experiences would mean that the game could be returned to the kids. After all, when we follow the evolution of hockey from shinny, bantam, high school, and college to the National Hockey League, it doesn't always seem like progress. Wouldn't we be better off if the game continued to be about fun and freedom of movement? Does the structured, competitive element really improve the game? Are we better off than we were on the sandlots, in the deserted gyms, or on the frozen ponds?

Actually, psychologists, philosophers, and educators agree that play, physical well-being (training), and competition teach important lessons to our young people, who, when left to their own devices, do not always reach the most helpful conclusions. For instance, in his informative study of the history of sport, *Sports and Freedom,* Ronald A. Smith describes the soap opera that accompanied the development of collegiate athletics. His stories are not the stuff legends are made of, at least not positive legends. Smith chronicles the initially unbridled passion of those college students who imported games from England and Western Europe, created their own rules, and imbued these hybrids with the competitiveness of the American character. Students ran these athletic teams with literally no guidance or interference from adults. The college faculties did not understand the games and there were no professional coaches or athletic directors. The students were left to figure things out for themselves. The results: Teams used mild forms of extortion to fund their enterprise. They bought top performers for their teams and developed a culture in which losing was synonymous with failure.

Some college teams hired their own professional coaches, out of their own funds, to give themselves a competitive edge. Winning became so much the issue, and sport competition threatened the academic program to such an extent, that the college administrators and faculties entered the dialogue and organized total programs. Universities implemented formal schedules (Wednesdays and Saturdays) to protect sacrosanct academic time and hired full-time coaches and athletic administrators. Historians noted that before too long the college football coaches' names would be more recognizable to the average student than that of the college president. This all transpired more than one hundred years ago, just before the turn of the last century. A decade later, in the early 1900s, the NCAA was formed to institutionalize the structure of these games.

These stories of manipulation and greed are not irrefutable evidence that children cannot manage their own affairs; rather, they are indications that the noble amateurism we long for may be more myth than reality. Children do have a way of working through issues when there is no adult presence to act as referee or source of authority and arbitration. Still, when playing on their own, children are likely to miss the opportunities for challenge and support that competent adults can orchestrate. Play, while important, does not offer the same environment for the engraving of proper habits that structured activities do. Our memories of games of shinny and sandlot pick-up may suggest that the world was a better place then, but chances are they are idealized versions of the past, our own personal halcyon days.

Unfortunately, as with the experience of the Greeks, many Americans have experienced athletic competition as a source of problems. Our games sometimes seem unable to embrace the amateur ideal we associate with the early Olympic competitions or even the sports of our youth. Clearly, our memories are more selective than reflective of the truth. The ideal of the amateur athlete in Hellenic Greece was the response to the felt need for heroes in that society. Ronald Smith cites ancient philosophers like Euripides who criticized these athletes for being spoiled and self-absorbed, guilty of believing they were far more important than they were. Are these examples of athletics producing or revealing flaws in the human character or of the absence of appropriate guidance and coaching? Remember, for every Babe Ruth, there is a Lou Gehrig.

Smith also reminds us that the heads of schools included athletics in the curriculum as activities that "would mold the characters as well as the forms of youth, that would brighten and quicken the intellectual faculties, giving energy to every action of mind as well as body; these [sports] should be as much a part of education as the teaching of the classics or any branch of studies." Educators have always seen the potential and the power of sport as a vehicle for instruction. The problem is that American sport has taken the British model of recreation (amateurism) and overlaid it with the competitive approach of those who are paid to compete (professional model). Charlie Brown's Snoopy summarized the feeling of most American athletes when he declared, "It doesn't matter if you win or lose, until you lose!"

Consequently, American coaches have always struggled with their concept of sport because it was borrowed and then reconstituted with a different cultural perspective. Americans wanted new challenges, new approaches, and new ways to compete. So, only those who understand how to balance the ideal of the amateur ethic (the mythical way sport used to be) with the need for gratification through victory (the attitude that brought glory as well as disgrace to professional sports through the last century) have been successful as coaches and as mentors. The challenge is to create environments in which both mastery of the appropriate habits and performance are valued and pursued equally. The relationship between these objectives should not be stated as an either/or proposition. Teams and programs that take care of the issues of character and habit, environments that foster the ethics and morals of the amateur spirit—to play the game with dignity, integrity, and respect—are among the most successful on the fields, courts, rinks, mats, and tracks.

Analyzing the Formal Structure

The Character and Sport Initiative has taken the pulse of many programs by asking athletic directors and coaches to identify the formal structure in their programs. To do so, they completed (1) a "Snapshot Assessment" of their own program, and (2) an "Identification of Program Stakeholders" profile. Our efforts were aimed at two objectives. First, we wanted to gauge how healthy or balanced these teams were. Second, we believed that this particular assessment tool would reinforce for coaches the importance of identifying the formal structure of their athletic programs.

The Snapshot Assessment

The Assessment (see Figure 5.1) provides a brief overview of a program by examining the program's characteristics. These characteristics include: (1) strengths, problems and issues; (2) the coach's approach to mastery and performance issues; (3) the methodology for making use of important opportunities to teach character, self-efficacy, and positive habits; and (4) commitment to its sense of mission.

Our analysis of responses from coaches and program administrators has taught us the following:

1. Coaches are rarely proactive about inviting others who are a part of the formal structure to participate in the sport process through goal setting, helpful communication, or role definition.

2. Coaches and athletic administrators rarely think that mission statements for teams or programs are needed if the larger organization (league, school, etc.) has one.

3. Many programs have problems and issues with "winning and performance" because of expectations, and these issues lead to negative reinforcement by parents, coaches, and schools.

4. Many programs are plagued by the adolescent focus on "self," which makes "Respect for Opponents" and "Commitment to Team" more challenging goals.

5. Fewer coaches than the CSI staff would have anticipated are as aware of their opportunities to mentor as they are of their responsibilities to teach the game.

The Snapshot Assessment clearly identified a lack of shared values as the greatest source of disagreement and frustration, almost as important as dealing with adolescent developmental issues. More on that later. There is one other finding that deserves attention and some discussion. In the Assessment, we asked coaches to rank in order the characteristics "you would want your players to think of when they remember you." Responses fell clearly into four categories which we at CSI would label "Excellent," "Good," "Fair," and "Poor." From the respondents' point of view, the categories could be labeled "Yes" (i.e., I want to be remembered that way)," "It's OK to be remembered that way," "Not Really," and "Please, No!" The responses were grouped as follows:

"Yes"	"OK"	"Not Really"	"Please, No!"
Fair	Respectful	Tough	Feared
Respected	Organized	Loved	
Knowledgeable	Consistent		
Caring/Compassionate			

FIGURE 5.1. The Snapshot Assessment

The CSI Snapshot Assessment is designed to give you a brief overview of your team/athletic program.

Age _____ ☐ M ☐ F

Please check all that apply:

☐ Current Athlete ☐ Teacher/Coach ☐ Parent ☐ Former Athlete

☐ Official ☐ Youth Program Director

☐ School Administrator: ☐ Elem. ☐ Secondary ☐ College

Program Characteristics: Regardless of policies and mission statements, how do you think the following characteristics influence your program (the sport experience within your school or organization). Check each characteristic be it either a strength, a problem/issue or a non-issue.

Characteristics	Strengths	Problem/Issue	Not an Issue—N/A
Winning/Performance			
Mastery/Fundamentals			
Fun/Enjoyment			
Respect for Opponent			
Responsibility/Commitment to Team			
Appreciation for the Game			
Positive Reinforcement (parents, coaches, school/organization in general)			
Respect for Self			
Fairness			
Honor			
Accountability (logical consequences for inappropriate behavior)			

Individual Characteristics: Rank in order characteristics you would want your players (coaches/players if you are an athletic/program director) to think of when they remember you. 1 = most desired; 10 = least desired.

Caring/compassionate	_____	Fair	_____
Tough	_____	Respected	_____
Organized	_____	Loved	_____
Knowledgeable	_____	Feared	_____
Respectful	_____	Consistent	_____

Responsibilities/Opportunities: Check the frequency with which you use each situation/experience as a teaching opportunity:

Responsibilities/Opportunities	Always	Sometimes	Seldom
Significant (big game) victories			
Significant (big game) defeats			
Negative parent involvement			
Team cuts			
Free time before practice			
Free time after practice			
Individual's failure to perform			
Incidence of profanity			
Practice planning			
Lateness to practice			
Bus/van rides			
High profile (pro sport) negative moments			
High profile (pro sport) positive moments			
Performance anxiety			
Penalties			
Lack of playing time			
Loss of coach's temper or composure			
Same treatment of less/more talented athletes			
Goal setting			

Short Answers:

Does your philosophy (purpose) of sport complement your school/athletic program/organization's stated mission? If yes, how? If no, why not?

Do you often get frustrated with your role as coach? If yes, why? If no, why not?

Does your program equally value process and outcome? If yes, how? If no, why not?

In our debriefing time with coaches, we pressed them on why "respected" was preferred more than "respectful," and why "loved" gets grouped with "tough" and "feared" as characteristics that have a pejorative connotation for these coaches. Some responded (defensively), saying that if the questionnaire had included "loving" instead of "loved," it would have been a more popular choice. The "respect" question may be a clue to the issues of the "respect for team" and "opponents" problems cited earlier. Coaches are always slightly embarrassed by their ranking of these items and agree that they have more to think about in this relationship.

Identifying Program Stakeholders

When most people think of sports we focus on the two opposing teams. However, is it important to include others who have important roles to play in our athletic programs at all levels? Who else influences the outcomes of games? Parents, officials, fans, administrators, teachers, trainers, and those who ready the equipment and the playing surfaces. There are dozens of others who have a stake in the outcome of the game or match, and these stakeholders need to be a part of our thinking and planning in any thoughtful approach to sport.

While few would disagree that all these people play a part in their sports experience, few understand the importance of requiring these disparate groups to engage in the same process of declaring their values that the athletes and coaches do. Miscommunication, criticism, and problems result from lack of agreement about what's important and why it's important. Finding common ground begins with the process of identifying the formal structure and working from there to find those values and goals that are compatible with those best represented by the formal structure.

As part of the CSI program, we ask athletic directors, coaches, and parents to complete the "Identification of Program Stakeholders" profile. This short inventory asks participants to reflect on who they believe make up the formal structure of the athletic program. Also we ask what the competing motivations may be among the adults in the formal structure. The following flow chart (Figure 5.2) presents the questions and illustrates the responses we received from a recent conference with secondary school coaches and athletic directors.

Stakeholders as Leadership Educators

Significant research has been performed on models of leadership for young people, and the CSI staff sees important parallels between being a coach/stakeholder and being a leadership educa-tor. Many businesses have adopted the coaching model for per-sonnel training and staff development and the desired outcomes —performance, self-discipline, perseverance, integrity, and hon-esty—are nearly identical. So it seems reasonable that what applies in one field should apply to the other. Leadership trainers stress the following characteristics in successful programs:

1. Consistent standards and values (common ground)

2. Cooperative learning

3. Time for self-reflection

4. Informative rather than controlling behavior by adults

5. Positive adult models

6. Structured progression of roles and responsibilities

7. Extrinsic rewards

8. Rites of passage (clearly delineated)

9. Performance feedback

10. Regular practice

All leadership educators agree that appropriate balance is the key to a positive experience. Young people respond well to challenges if the challenges are balanced by support. This is the lesson of the Sport Information Questionnaire and the Snapshot Assessment for both the coaches and the athletes. This balance is

FIGURE 5.2 Identification of Program Stakeholders

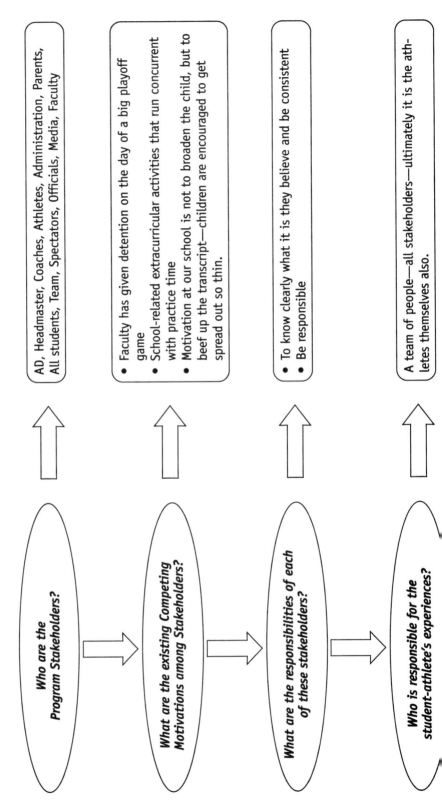

Who are the Program Stakeholders? → AD, Headmaster, Coaches, Athletes, Administration, Parents, All students, Team, Spectators, Officials, Media, Faculty

What are the existing Competing Motivations among Stakeholders? →
- Faculty has given detention on the day of a big playoff game
- School-related extracurricular activities that run concurrent with practice time
- Motivation at our school is not to broaden the child, but to beef up the transcript—children are encouraged to get spread out so thin.

What are the responsibilities of each of these stakeholders? →
- To know clearly what it is they believe and be consistent
- Be responsible

Who is responsible for the student-athlete's experiences? → A team of people—all stakeholders—ultimately it is the athletes themselves also.

what the researchers in sport psychology cite as the components needed for "flow performances" in athletics. Other notable sport philosophers conclude that the appropriate balance between these components lead to greater self-efficacy and better performance. This balance, like the blending of emphasis on both performance and mastery, is the potential that can be realized when thoughtfully reflective, caring adult's mentor and coach young people in sports.

Unfortunately, in spite of this knowledge, coaches continue to struggle with this equation or neglect the not-so-obvious people who have important roles in the formal structure who could bring consistency and better adult modeling to their children's sport experience. Equally significant is the inability to keep sports in the proper perspective, a failure that leads to conflicting values, contamination, and frustration for all involved in the activity.

We have come to realize a variety of stakeholder influences that have become most problematic in sports today:

1. Pressure to begin competition at too young an age

2. Pressure to specialize too early—focus on one sport

3. Pressure to win at all costs

4. Absence of joy and fun in the endeavor

5. Presence of sport violence

6. Presence of negative parental interference

7. Presence of too many coaches (youth and high school) who are not sensitive to the responsibilities for character development in their athletes

Clearly, these pressures and negative influences result from misconceptions about what is expected and what is important—what really matters. They not only create unhealthy situations for young people, but they also confuse them. Whenever adults do not act as adults are "supposed to," it disappoints and unsettles children. The idealized adult coach is supposed to protect the sanctity of the team and to represent the consistency, honesty, integrity, and care that young players want and need to emulate. Adults who behave like children, on the sidelines or in the stands, communicate nothing positive to sport participants. Emphasis on winning above all else and at all costs puts the focus on the outcome rather than on the all-important process. A life-long academic and athletic administrator put it well when he said, "I have always felt that it was my primary responsibility to teach them to appreciate the game and to learn to play it respectfully." Winning games is the by-product of an enlightened approach to sports, not the sole objective.

Contamination occurs when adults put "respected" before "respectful." When parents are more concerned about the outcome of a contest than the experience of positive competition, they place blame on others. It may relieve the pain of embarrassment or the sting of disappointment, but it represents behavior we would not want our children to imitate. "Losing it" on the official teaches athletes lack of self-control. Haranguing a team for lack of performance guarantees that athletes will focus more on your behavior than theirs. Allowing dangerous or unsportsmanlike conduct to pass for toughness or competitive spirit will lead to a compromising of the values that make sport worthwhile. When concern for final outcome becomes more important than concern for the participants on both sides of the field or scorer's table, perspective has been lost and responsibility has been abdicated.

The media send our young people clear messages about what is important—dynasties, routs, streaks, dominance. Champions are celebrated. Those who try to beat the system get the attention. Big contracts, signing bonuses, headlines. Those who lose console themselves. Winners who are disappointed are the worst kind of losers. Brawls, flagrant fouls, and cheap shots are tolerated, even encouraged by many in sports.

The messages are at least consistent. But this coverage is for sport entertainers, professional athletes, our modern gladiators, who play for pay. The contamination at the youth and high school level is the result of coaches and parents not taking time to reflect on what are the ends to which sports are the means. Adults who assault the confidence of our young do worse damage than the news writers and television commentators. Grownups who belittle or neglect the sacred trust of coaching are far guiltier than the pro athletes for setting an example that cripples our sport. Sadly, most of the damage is done by adults with good intentions and a history of contamination in their own sport backgrounds. Like hazing, sport contamination is a vicious cycle that is passed along by those who were originally wronged or by parents and coaches who create pressure innocently by asking the wrong questions and emphasizing the wrong behaviors.

If we could return to the "sandlot" ideal, we wouldn't have to worry about early specialization, overemphasis on winning, or inappropriate adults. There was no "formal structure" to be concerned about, and few incidences of violence. The game was played for fun, and others seldom treated the participants badly or insensitively. Kids worked at their own pace. They learned important lessons about cooperation and competition, but they did not have the benefit of the wisdom and experience of caring adults as mentors and adult friends. "Reclaiming the purpose of sport" is not about giving the game back to the kids by abandoning them or leaving them to their own devices on the playgrounds. As caring adults we have the privilege of interpreting, leading, and sharing our knowledge and love of the game with them as they explore their physical and emotional worlds. Children and adolescents need adult mentors who are not their parents to help them in the maturation process. Coaches can provide the consistency and objectivity that are not always easy for parents to offer.

(6)

Identifying Team and Program Core Virtues

Things which matter most must never be at the mercy of things that matter least.

— Goethe

The first-year coach of a competitive Division I athletic program began his remarks at the team's annual post-season banquet by summarizing the high points of the year for the parents in attendance. He explained that the most significant event was the creation of the program's "credo." The team had met in the pre-season, had discussed their individual values and goals, their hopes for the team, and their expectations of their team-mates. The coach then created a set of commandments, a "credo," to guide and govern the team during the season. These agreements became their mission statement and represented their shared values and the char-acter habits that would lead them to the realization of their goals.

The commitments tacitly made by this mission statement covered much of the familiar athletic ground: team, enjoyment, discipline, hard work, perseverance, loyalty, and self-control. What was unique and most important to this team was that they had made the effort to write it down. They had made a formal declaration of what their identity as a team would be for that season. They publicly declared their willingness to put the team's well being ahead of personal goals and to support teammates by acts of commission (partner exercises) and omission (abstinence from unhealthy behavior). They had a formal document that symbolized their seriousness of purpose, their word that they agreed on what was truly important. As the night progressed and every graduating senior spoke about his four years on the team, each noted the importance of the "credo" as a galvanizing force throughout the season.

Stories like these are far too rare. First, few coaches appreciate the need to write down what is absolutely clear to them. Could writing down a team's foundational beliefs, its ethos, actually result in better performance? Second, few athletic or school administrators see the important connections between their school's mission statement (if they have one) and what happens in their athletic programs. Why would anyone assume that the team's mission statement would differ from or be enhanced by the school's? Finally, few coaches or administrators see the need to involve participants in creating a set of commitments that go beyond training rules. What could these athletes possibly add to the dialogue that we (adults) have not considered or included? Consequently, ideas or views are shared informally, without commitment; and, often, the subsequent actions of the team or its members are not indicative of what was collectively approved in the pre-season.

What is more troubling are the by-products of not declaring oneself, individually or as a group. Again, the business analogy can be helpful. Most businesses ask all employees to sign a code of ethics, a document stating that they will deal honestly in relationships with vendors, avoid conflicts of interest in financial areas, and otherwise act ethically. Other businesses go even further by asking employees to sign a credo or mission statement in which, for example, they commit to treating customers with respect and courtesy, upholding the company's quality standards, and the like.

Imagine what can happen if managers are not successful in convincing their employees to declare their support for these documents. Criticism flows all too easily when only one group in the formal structure is required to declare itself. Moreover, all who declare their opinion, publicly or formally, risk criticism because their views are "out there" for all to see and evaluate. The point is this: As long as your views are not public, you are free to take any position, have any opinion, or represent any point of view on a given issue. Once you declare yourself, you have lost that anonymity.

Consider the case of the parent fan. There is an instructive story of a benevolent Little League coach who assumed that all his players were "all stars," were capable of representing the team, and deserved to play. But only he had declared himself. He revealed his values, his philosophy, by substituting players to provide everyone with playing opportunities. The parents, who had risked nothing, felt comfortable challenging the coach's decision because their own values were not being examined. They had not been required or invited to "declare" their values (although they may have exposed them through their comments).

Had the coach explained his thoroughly understandable philosophy on playing time and asked parents for their reaction, he probably would have received support for his commitment to all the boys on the team. Because he did not, he had opened the door that allowed fans to criticize without the fear of being exposed. His decisions and values were being examined, not theirs.

Just as not taking advantage of the opportunity to mentor a player who has committed an unnecessary foul or has had a poor practice is a mistake, neglecting to encourage players, parents, and school officials to declare their values represents an even greater missed opportunity. Mission statements and coaching philosophies, when shared with parents and administrators, can generate positive dialogue and lead to the identification of positive values and core virtues for both a program and a team.

Inviting those who are part of the formal structure to reveal their values is as fundamental as covering the rules of competition. All significant stakeholders should make their values and expectations known to others in this relationship. Athletics, like businesses or classrooms, function better when the participants—leaders, followers, and observers—communicate clearly with one another. Coaches have a responsibility to articulate to parents, administrators, and sport participants the philosophy and the values that they will bring to the program. Parents have a right to know what coaches view as the their responsibility to the young people in their care. Athletes also should know whom they are playing for and what that person's expectations and modus operandi are. A clearly expressed mission statement begins a dialogue that encourages all to declare openly "what matters" in this activity.

If, as a parent, I am eager to have my child involved with a "win at all costs" program, and I learn before the season my child's coach-to-be has a "play everyone" approach, I will have the opportunity to discuss our conflicting values in a private and timely manner. Coaches are performing a service (even volunteer coaches). They have the right to know about the expectations of parents and participants. Until agreements are written down or expressed openly, those involved have not fulfilled their obligations to one another and to the spirit of collaboration. Good coaching, like good teaching, should be viewed as a partnership in which coaches complement and supplement the work of the schools and the parents in developing children's skills, positive habits, and healthy perspectives on self and others. Therefore, coaches who create a process for identifying the team's core virtues, as T. J. Williams did, are meeting the needs of all constituencies. Such processes may take time, but they pay important dividends and help everyone reflect on what sports ought to be.

The idea of declaring a program's core virtues is not new. As we noted earlier, a growing number of large businesses have made the use of guiding principles attractive when they unveiled their credos as a way of evaluating any and all of the company's decisions. If the activity supported the credo, it was appropriate and reasonable.

While this seems obvious, many programs have not taken the time to establish any agreements, and if they have, they may not have gone beyond individual "values" in their discussion. Everyone has an opinion or a point of view on almost every subject. Thinking something or having a strong feeling about it does not make it true, enduring, or important. Values, as we learned in Chapter 2, are individually driven and may or may not be virtuous. Values are more compelling than views, but they may not address what is ultimately important, what our young people ought to learn in their meaningful experience with sport. A credo, which serves to identify and emphasize virtuous behavior, provides a foundation for expectations of behavior. An expressing of one's values is a good place to begin, but it does not take the place of having a team experience or a program grounded in the virtues that have defined excellence, fairness, and sportsmanship for centuries.

The 30-Second Commercial—
Declaring, Analyzing and Aligning Core Virtues

We asked athletic directors and coaches the following question: "If your school were to come up in conversation, internally or externally, and the subject of your team or athletic department came up, what would you want others to say about it?" This question asks the participant to declare what he or she believes matters most in the athletic program. This exercise is called *The 30-Second Commercial* because it asks athletic program stakeholders to advertise their athletic program in a brief, clear, and concise manner. The following flow chart (Figure 6.1) presents the questions and illustrates the responses we received from a recent conference of secondary school athletic directors and coaches.

Figure 6.1 The 30-Second Commercial

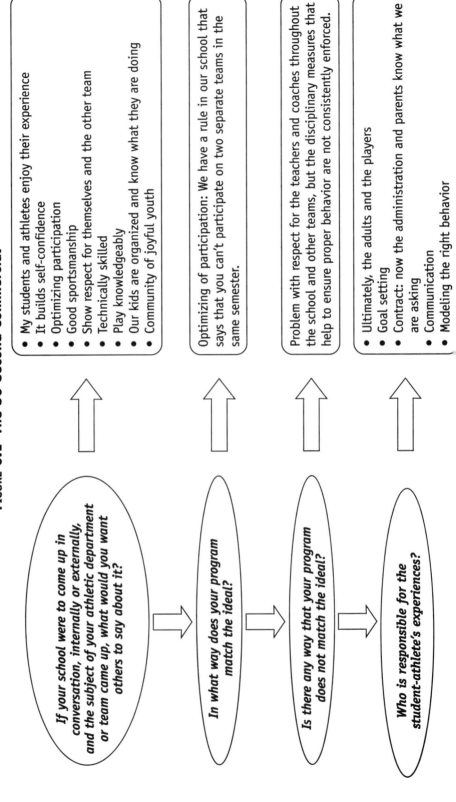

If your school were to come up in conversation, internally or externally, and the subject of your athletic department or team came up, what would you want others to say about it?

- My students and athletes enjoy their experience
- It builds self-confidence
- Optimizing participation
- Good sportsmanship
- Show respect for themselves and the other team
- Technically skilled
- Play knowledgeably
- Our kids are organized and know what they are doing
- Community of joyful youth

In what way does your program match the ideal?

Optimizing of participation: We have a rule in our school that says that you can't participate on two separate teams in the same semester.

Is there any way that your program does not match the ideal?

Problem with respect for the teachers and coaches throughout the school and other teams, but the disciplinary measures that help to ensure proper behavior are not consistently enforced.

Who is responsible for the student-athlete's experiences?

- Ultimately, the adults and the players
- Goal setting
- Contract: now the administration and parents know what we are asking
- Communication
- Modeling the right behavior

The second part of this exercise asks: "In what way does your program match the ideal?" In other words, are the stakeholders in your program doing what they want others to think they are doing? The third part asks: "Is there any way that your program doesn't match the ideal?" This question asks the stakeholder to analyze any areas that may need improvement. Finally, the exercise asks: "What can you do to adjust the program so it can be in greater alignment?"

By answering this question, stakeholders realize the degree of alignment between what they would ideally want for the program, and what is really happening. This exercise prompts athletic directors, coaches, parents, and other community stakeholders to put the ideals of the program out on the table and to work on sharing and achieving common ground.

Core Virtues in Action

Integrity

Coaches and administrators who are assessing how their programs would rate on a core-virtues measurement must identify how character habits manifest themselves in the program or team concept. Is integrity explained, practiced, valued? Do all stakeholders understand the same operational definitions of integrity, or does it depend on the circumstances, or on how important the competition is, or on whose child is involved? When Edwin Delattre describes integrity as "a single consistency throughout," he is talking about the benefits of living a life in which positive values and core virtues, a person's guiding principles, must always be the filter for decision making. Many have said that the difference between discipline and self-discipline is that self-discipline is in evidence when actions are performed without any expectations of recognition or reward. Whether the official detected the violation or not, the coach who practices integrity responds to the situation immediately. Integrity is demonstrated by right action always. Integrity does not depend on outcomes or consequences; it determines them.

Respect

As far as our society has gone in the direction of promoting outcome (winning) versus process (personal growth), there are indications that many adults appreciate the importance of justice and equal opportunity in their programs. "Living in the skin" of others is not easy, but more people are talking about access to sport opportunity than there were when we (as authors) were young. Ninth-grade teams, second junior-varsity programs, no-cut policies on lower-level teams, two-inning participation rules, and more equal gender opportunity all suggest that many adults in sport have made justice a higher priority.

Remembering that children are still children, not simply smaller versions of adults, is a start. Putting one's own needs as the adult stakeholder in the context of the other participants' needs is an important next step. When the coaches of a traveling all-star baseball team of eight- and nine-year-olds are overheard complaining that an eight-year-old player is "so immature and will not give 120 percent," one wonders about the centrality of justice in some programs. When players languish on the bench with little emotional support, one must assume there is little compassion or empathy in the coach's approach. Respect for parents, athletes, the program, opponents, officials, and self is the most obvious indicator of justice. However, it is difficult to know what other people expect or need if you do not ask them or make the effort to learn.

When we explained the CSI concept to a well-known women's coach and asked her for a reaction, she responded that her greatest frustration and deepest sadness in sports resulted from seeing a loss of respect, from her team and from spectators, for the opponents. She was uncertain whether this lack of concern for the opposing team was the result of selfishness, higher stakes competition, the coaches' own trash-talking as a form of motivation, or all of the above. She felt we needed to help her athletes and fans understand that respect for the opponent is as fundamental to a positive sports experience as respect for the game and respect for self.

It occurred to us that pre-game talks that characterize the opponents as "not belonging on the same field with us," or "unworthy of our best efforts," cannot be helpful to any athlete working to understand the delicate balance between being competitive and being cooperative. Athletes need to remember that when opponents enter a contest with healthy respect for one another, sport wins. This is an important step in beginning to reclaim its purpose.

Courage

The athlete is not the only person in the formal structure who should value and practice the virtue of courage. If courage means "acting on what is morally responsible without rashness or cowardice," it is fundamentally about having the wherewithal to do the right thing. This relates to the work ethic, personal discipline, support of teammates, responsible "fanship," and willingness to risk. The most difficult time for courageous behavior is when others expect or encourage you to do what you believe is wrong. It takes courage to say no to adults who are asking you to act without regard for integrity or justice. It takes courage to allow your child to learn the hard lessons of competition. It takes courage to focus attention on all in your care, not just the gifted ones. It takes courage to commit to principles and philosophies that do not ensure short-term gratification or popularity. It takes courage to take the long-view. What happens in this game or the next is certainly not as crucial as what is learned in the experience. Teaching positive lessons and modeling right behavior takes courage from all stakeholders.

Moderation/Balance

Tied closely to the patience and the perspective necessary for one to act with courage are balance and moderation. "Nothing to excess" sums it up succinctly. Unfortunately, excess defines our society. "You can't have too much of a good thing"; "you can't be too thin or too rich"; "you can't win often enough." Balance and moderation have been forgotten in many aspects of our lives and in many of our sport programs, even those ostensibly organized for the benefit of children. When a youth-soccer coach is criticized because her four- and five-year-old players are not practicing often or working hard enough to win, one must question the place of moderation in this community. When pee wee travel teams play 60 to 75 games in a season, one should worry about balance as well as justice. When adults lose their perspective and treat a youth sports activity as though it were the most important thing they or the participants do, moderation has been lost as a goal. It should not surprise anyone that the greatest dropout rate for youth in sports occurs before high school. Eleven-, twelve- and thirteen-year-olds leave in droves, many claiming that the activity has ceased to be fun. We wonder if they begin to question whether the game is really for or about them.

Americans are not especially good about balance when it comes to eating, exercising, or working. Therefore, coaches and parents need to be even more sensitive than usual to the contaminating or destructive consequences of excess in their children's lives. In fact, coaches have the unusual opportunity to present to their athletes a model of an adult who can balance tasks and responsibilities without obsessing about them. Children learn through imitation of the actions of both the adult and peer models who populate their world. Would you be surprised to learn that the most unruly teams were coached by adults who had not achieved this balance in their own lives?

Care and Compassion

Last, we come to care and compassion, the hallmarks of the educator coach. A person of good character has achieved a level of accommodation with self that allows for sharing and caring. The "completed" person has become comfortable enough with his or her self to be able to provide for another's emotional needs.

Respecting others starts with respecting self. Caring is easier when one feels cared about. It is difficult to take another's point of view when you are totally focused on your own needs. All have the right to expect something for themselves from any activity, but the healthy or virtuous program ranks high on the scale of altruism and support. This is part of being in another's skin, part of being concerned with justice, and part of being willing to do the right thing, always.

Putting it all Together

These core virtues are synonymous with the character of a team or program. They symbolize the group's shared commitment to personal excellence as well as performance. Actually, taking care of character issues is one of the best ways of addressing the performance issue. Performance and perspective are not mutually exclusive; on the contrary, they are mutually supportive. Explanations that are dualistic (based on either/or reasoning) in nature or approach are generally too simplistic—they reduce complex situations to unrealistically easy choices. Teams that focus on the character piece are in no way prevented from access to winning. Good performance becomes a by-product of self-disciplined teams that recognize the importance of balance and care in their programs.

We know a person who coaches what is arguably the most consistently successful high school program in the country. His athletes graduate from his program and enjoy equal success at the highest level of collegiate competition. When I asked him what was the most important thing he had learned in the last few years, his response surprised and pleased me. "I discovered that I had been over-training my athletes for years. I also learned that giving them days off on a more regular basis and keeping practices shorter and more fun worked wonders for me and the kids."

A good exercise for stimulating discussion on the importance of interdependence is the twelve-foot wall and dodge ball gambit. A group engages in a game of dodge ball until there is one person remaining, and they follow up that activity with the task of making sure all members of their group get over a twelve-foot wall. After both exercises have been completed, the members of the group are asked to describe what happened in each game. Most agree that dodge ball is an activity that emphasizes individual skills, is only cooperative to the extent that players use one another to their advantage, and rewards the most capable person. Deeper analysis might lead to the observation that the person who ends up getting the most practice is the person with the most skill to begin with. Others will make comparisons to Little League sports and competitive athletics in general. The discussion may lead to the resultant confidence for the winner and the increased self-worth of those who played well.

The conclusions about the twelve-foot wall game are polar opposites. This is a game about cooperation and collaboration. Leaders are chosen or they emerge, and the group assesses its abilities and weaknesses in order to create a plan that will benefit all involved. There is a winner only if the group as a whole is successful, and then all team members feel equally good about the outcome. We might assume that a "twelve-foot wall society" would surely be a better place to live and a better model for our programs than the winner-takes-all scenario of scatter dodge. This overlooks one important point: The leaders who emerged to ensure success in the wall-scaling task either honed their skills in some type of competitive program or were able to utilize those who had, for the benefit of the group. In other words, both competition and collaboration are necessary in our society. One without the other would not provide the balance we seek.

Successful programs are generally coached or administered by adults who understand the importance of modeling consistently responsible behavior. They do not engage in senseless tirades on the sidelines. They do not berate officials. They do not humiliate their players. They show respect for their players and their program. They have a balanced approach to winning and losing. They are fierce competitors and they may hate to lose. They usually do not take it personally. They realize that all aspects of their programs are interconnected.

Most importantly, they make sure that all the significant stakeholders involved with a program's formal structure are aware of the specifics of the program's espoused values and core virtues. They communicate with players, parents, and administrators. Theirs are the model programs, in part because the people in the program understand, share, and believe in the virtues that are the foundation of the program. When all stakeholders have signed off on the core virtues and have been encouraged to declare themselves in the process, team building and support garnering come much more easily.

The coach whose team created their formal credo cited at the beginning of this chapter won the New England Regionals and the Eastern Regionals. They sent the largest contingent to the NCAA tournament in their program's history, and they returned home with a healthy share of All-Americans. The team members also felt the season was the one in which they had learned the most important lessons for life.

Application

(7)

Walking the Talk—
Building Core Virtues in
Athletic Programs

They don't need just information; they need meaningful information. They don't need just knowledge; they need knowledge that makes sense and inspires belief. They need knowledge that helps them understand why learning and living are worthwhile.
Kevin Ryan and James Cooper—*Those Who Can, Teach*

For our athletic programs to be truly character-based, it is essential that we not only know and value the good, but that we also aspire to act on the established core virtues in the program's mission statement. When parents, coaches, athletic directors, and other administrators "walk the talk," their actions speak volumes to our athletes about the importance of developing enduring character habits. The mission statement becomes an important document. It binds those involved in an athletic program together in a common purpose and gives participants an opportunity to declare what they think is important about the program. This can provide strong and compelling motivation to act according to the mission's tenets.

The Mission Statement as a Guide for Ethical Conduct

The mission statement conveys what a group believes to be of significant worth and value. If people are serious about using it, they ought to be able to get the most out of the document. The mission statement is a tool that helps guide and analyze every action taken by a coach or athletic director. It also makes clear the expectations for student-athlete and parent behavior. When you know and fully understand the program's mission, and have chosen to value the meanings and intentions of the compelling language within, then the next logical step is to act according to the mission. The document serves as a simple reminder to do the right thing. When an ethical problem is presented on or off the field, go back to the statement. If the mission is clearly stated and understood, there is no moral dilemma. The right decision is already known. Acting on the moral decision is essential. If an action doesn't reflect the mission, then it shouldn't be taken.

The mission statement can be a wonderful decision-making tool. Whenever you are faced with indecision, refer back to the purpose and vision of the mission statement. If the action doesn't fit, you don't do it. This takes the ambiguity out of the process. It also decreases the emotional response to the action. Most people are aware of what they ought to do, but sometimes allow their emotions to get in the way. The danger comes from the fact that emotional states are in flux. They are valuable as information, just as any other part of any context in which we find ourselves. However, we must recognize what needs to be done. For example, if the mission espouses respect for teammates, there should be no question when substituting players regardless of the score or climate of the game.

A variety of high school athletic directors told us that they ask prospective new coaches to read and reflect on the athletic program's mission statement and program guidelines. They ask each applicant if the program's mission and guidelines are something he or she will value and act upon. If the answer is yes, then the prospective coach declares his or her allegiance to uphold these principles. If there is any doubt, then there probably isn't a good match between the applicant and the athletic program. Unfortunately, as Matt King, superintendent of the Wellesley, MA, public schools suggests, as the expectations for good coaches go up, the pool of available coaches who meet those expectations decreases.

In many public secondary schools, one-third or more of the coaching staff are not teachers. Some coaches and athletic directors argue that there aren't enough good, experienced coaching candidates available. There are at least two reasons for this phenomenon: expansion in the number of teams and sports offered and increasing demands on coaches. Therefore "beggars can't be choosers," or so some administrators think.

However, having "warm bodies" fill coaching vacancies without regard to their influence on young people is a threat to the program's mission. The problem in hiring a "warm body" who may have difficulty following the team and program objectives is that the would-be coach may do harm to the athletes' overall experience. Good athletic programs make every effort available to find a suitable coach. Parents who volunteer to coach their sons' or daughters' under-ten youth-soccer team may be well-intentioned, but may not necessarily be aware of and willing to do what it takes to ensure a positive experience for the athletes they serve.

Creating a Character-Based Mission

Following a carefully constructed mission statement obliges all those involved in the athletic program to declare themselves. Therefore, it is important that all people who are participants in an athletic program—the stakeholders—have a say in the development of a mission. The stakeholders should represent every aspect of the community that is involved with the athletic program. There ought to be a commitment of time, energy, and other resources to create the declaration. It is not about whipping together three or four common goals. It is about spending the time necessary to develop, "word for word," meaningful and purposeful instruction about the athletic program. There may not be one hundred percent consensus. But even without full consensus, a written document will give some people pause before acting in a manner that may come back to haunt them. And ideally, it will inspire people to act in positive, ethical ways of their own accord.

The athletic program's mission ought to be very explicit— clearly defined and specific. Matt King claims that problems typically develop when there is a lack of shared understanding of expectations. Many stakeholders, especially parents, tend to bring to the table their implicit understandings of the purpose of interscholastic sports. These may be understood, but there can be a tremendous amount of dissatisfaction during the policy-making process. Mission development and modification deserve an open forum, a place where reasonable people can differ. Recall the statement by T.J Williams, cited earlier, that creating an appropriate mission can be the administrative equivalent of eating tinfoil.

Developing and applying core virtues through the mission statement is a progressive and sequential process. An acronym called the 5D's, as shown in Figure 7.1, can be instructive here. First, there must be **D**ialogue—the identification of core virtues. Second, after identifying the core virtues within your team or program, it is important to develop a consensus in **D**efining them—stating clearly what each means to the success of the program and what each looks like. Core virtues must then be **D**econstructed—broken down to their simplest terms. In other words, what do these virtues look like behaviorally? Fourth, core virtues and their application must be **D**eclared by the group to be of prime importance. Finally, group members must commit themselves to acting in accordance with these agreed-upon standards. They must go out and **D**o them!

FIGURE 7.1 The 5 D's of Core Value Construction

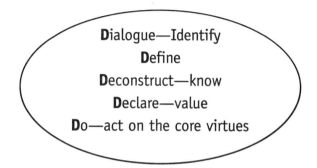

Dialogue—Identify
Define
Deconstruct—know
Declare—value
Do—act on the core virtues

Mission statements vary in their length, structure, and content. Several cardinal rules serve to support the creation of such a document. These guidelines, outlined in Figure 7.2, are necessary to the logical construction of the mission.

FIGURE 7.2. Characteristics of an Effective Mission Statement

Virtues and vision
Common language
Sense of purpose
Meaningful
Inspirational
Clear, concise — brevity
Action
Staying the course

Virtues and Vision

In order to create a truly effective mission, you must be able to determine how you want your program to look as a "finished product." How would you want to be known by others both inside and outside your program?

Common Language

It is essential for mission statements to have a common language, so that all participants/stakeholders can easily comprehend the expectations and ethos of the program. Core virtues ought to be expressed and defined in simple terms that everyone can understand. Virtues are the basis to a character-based program, so that there ought to be a convincing portrayal of what these habits mean and look like. Jeff Beedy, the founder and president of the Global Character Institute and The SportsPLUS program, claims

> It's better to keep it simple. It's helpful if you put
> these values [virtues] into behavioral terms so that
> when you are talking with your athletes, they actu-
> ally understand what the words mean. You might say
> to them, "look, we need to be more responsible." Or,
> "we need to be more respectful." But what does that
> mean to a player who grew up in a family who never
> taught him or her what respect or responsibility
> meant?

Explaining what a core virtue means and looks like by describing behaviors can be very instructive and informative, as the virtue can then be pictured in action. For example, The Independent School League (ISL), a grouping of private secondary schools in New England, has a general mission statement (shown below) that binds all the school's athletic programs.

Independent School League (ISL) Mission Statement

Players shall at all times represent themselves and their school with honor, proper conduct, and good sportsmanship. They shall understand that competitive rivalries are encouraged but that disrespect for opponents is unsportsmanlike and lessens the value of the rivalries. They shall confine the competitiveness of the game to the field, and in particular behave properly on the sidelines and in the locker rooms both before and after games.

It is important that the terms *honor, proper conduct,* and *good sportsmanship* are simply and clearly defined within each school and collectively throughout the league so that all stake-holders have a working knowledge of these virtues. The mission works when all know what honor, proper conduct and good sportsmanship look like, and when everyone values putting these ideas into practice.

Sense of purpose

The mission ought to be written affirmatively and positively— establishing the reasons for and value of participation in the program. This is about "why" people participate in the program— reasons like enjoyment, satisfaction or striving for excellence.

Meaningful

Virtues ought to be defined so they make sense to all the participants. Children, adolescents, and adults tend to remain focused on activities that hold some sense of significance for them. Virtues really matter when their action reflects the shared purpose of the group.

Inspirational

Good missions inspire belief and illustrate why participating in the endeavor is worth doing well. An inspiring mission statement instills faith and confidence in the value of participation and the worth of aspiring to the program's core virtues.

Clarity and Brevity

Good mission statements are clear and concise. From a mechanical perspective, the briefer a mission statement is, the clearer it should be to the coach, program director, athlete, and parent. It shouldn't be ambiguous or terribly detailed, but something you can easily understand. The mission statement of the athletic department at The Montclair Kimberley Academy in Montclair, New Jersey, is brief and concise. It consists of three words: (1) Opportunity, (2) Quality, and (3) Sportsmanship. Although there are only three words, each core virtue is carefully defined, espoused, and acted upon daily in MKA's athletic culture. The definitions are as follows:

- **Opportunity**—All students who wish to be on a team can be, if they are willing to adhere to the commitments required of them by the coach.

- **Quality**—Our goal is for every athlete, team, and coach to develop their talents to the fullest, and compete to the best of their ability.

- **Sportsmanship**—We believe that winning is not just achieved on a scoreboard, but also requires the highest standards of conduct from every athlete, coach, and spectator involved.

Action

Action is the real power behind core virtues. Knowing the contents of the mission statement and valuing them are not good enough. It is applying the core virtues in daily action, on and off the field, at home, and at school that really produces an enduring mission. Lisa Lahey cites Matt King's conception of an active core virtue: "A core value [virtue] must show up in people's behaviors. Most importantly, a core value [virtue] is woven into the fabric of decision-making within the school: a core value [virtue] drives decisions. If a core value [virtue] does not show up in behaviors, we take it to be more of an espoused value— what people would like to believe in. The first criteria [sic] then is that there needs to be consistency between actions and words in order for a core value [virtue] to have power."

Consistency between actions and words can happen only when coaches, program directors, parents, and student-athletes model the behavior suggested in the mission. The mission is present in every practice and every game. The aims of the program are discussed and modeled constantly. When actions are contrary to the words in the mission, there ought to be logical consequences for those behaviors.

The major challenge exists in acting on the mission statement. Every time Bob Bigelow speaks to a group of parents and coaches of young athletes, there is a continual nodding of heads in the audience, silently proclaiming "you are so right." He brings the awareness quotient up several notches in each community where he presents. Seldom do people outwardly challenge Bob's declaration of making youth sports in the best interests of the youth. Most parents would want that for their children and others in the community.

But if almost everybody agrees with Bob, why don't they take the action needed? Because it is hard for all of us at times to put our own self-interest, habits, and agendas aside for what is truly right. Change is not easy. Some may say, "You mean to say that we ought to actually live by the mission statement?" Others will say that there are far too many situations that invite interpretation. But, if a mission statement is clearly written and articulated, with meaningful and understandable definitions, and there is a process to measure and evaluate it, the need to interpret the document is drastically reduced. It clearly says what we aspire to as an athletic program. So in the heat of competition there really becomes no excuse for an athlete, coach, program director, or parent not to follow the mission. If "respect" is what the program is about, then we act either respectfully to teammates and opponents, or we don't. There is no middle ground. We should be willing to let the mission be enough to guide us.

Staying the Course

Following the letter of the mission sometimes causes internal resistance. For some people in the athletic program, the enacting of a mission invites a certain level of anxiety in that coaches and athletes are being held accountable for their actions. M. Walker Buckalew, an authority on teacher evaluation, raises two important questions: "Is the payoff worth the tension?" That question is best answered with another: "Is your institution's mission, and the young people whom that mission purports to serve, worth the leadership time and effort necessary to develop and sustain a mission position?" The new mission can be subtly sabotaged by veteran coaches who choose not to reflect on their purposes, by cynical coaches, or by less experienced coaches who have never been properly mentored.

Buckalew also states that "a coach may lose a game because her new consciousness of the mission's implications leads her to play marginal athletes longer than previously." Will those in charge of a program be willing and able to "stay the course" when some stakeholders find situations like this unacceptable?

Although many coaches are very reflective about their responsibilities and opportunities, there are some whose ideals exemplify something different from the core virtues espoused in the program. Some coaches may not be committed personally to the core virtues, but still represent the program's mission with their on-field behavior because they think that it is in the best interests of the athletes. It is important that coaches are clear on what the behavioral expectations of them are. If, as leaders, as long as coaches carry out their duties in the spirit of the mission, even though they may not "buy in" to these principles personally, we ought to be able to live with that. Most people are virtuous in varying degrees. However, Aristotle once said, "We become just by doing just acts . . . brave by doing brave acts." Some coaches may begin to act more virtuous by the habitual process of fulfilling their duties to the program.

Modifying the Mission Statement

Some coaches and athletic directors remark that their existing missions don't have enough teeth in them. One athletic director remarked that his program's mission statement is still on mimeographed paper. Of course, we want missions to be enduring. We also want them to be read, understood, acted upon, and modified when necessary. When the observed actions of players, coaches, and parents don't fit the words on paper, then it may be time to modify the mission. Programs that do not successfully implement their mission don't fall apart; they tend to fray over a period of time. Therefore, Jeff Beedy advises that the implementation of the athletic program's philosophy be continually reviewed. He says, "You need to have a model based on a philosophy. Your philosophy drives your practical affairs. It will tell you whether you have seniors playing on the junior varsity. It is going to tell you if you should be distributing playing time evenly or not. Revisit your educational model during the season in order to reinforce and support your philosophy." If there are issues with how the mission is carried out, then the policies and procedures of the program ought to be upgraded.

Although striving for excellence is mentioned in most athletic program missions as a core virtue, the question, "Is this what excellence means?" should be reflected upon with some regularity. If a program isn't the "best it can be," what changes can be made to ensure that high levels of enjoyment, satisfaction, and performance are consistently realized? This ought to be an ethical responsibility that begins with the adult leadership of the athletic program. Some teams run into talent pool problems and won-lost records tend to reverse themselves, but the top-down effort in the program continues to support the core virtue. The important question to ask here is: "If excellence is part of a program's mission, what can be done to improve this team in this situation?" Once we know what we want people to say about our program, how do we implement that in practice?

Measuring and Evaluating Virtue in Athletic Programs

Once the mission has been set in place, how do you and others determine and know that you are acting in accordance with the mission? How do we best measure virtue in our programs? If you can't measure the terms, maybe they aren't the right terms. A chief justice of the United States, discussing the concept of obscenity, once said, in effect, "I can't define it, but I know it when I see it." What is said about vice can also be said of virtue. There is no such thing as a pure, exacting evaluation tool to measure virtuous behavior. Human beings are complex and there are many confounding variables that make a total objective assessment unrealistic. However, we can roughly assign certain weight to certain behaviors. Marvin Berkowitz and the Character Education Partnership Assessment Committee suggest that there are some important questions (see Figure 7.3) that ought to be addressed prior to evaluating a character-based program.

FIGURE 7.3. A Primer for Evaluating a Character Education Initiative

1. Why do you want to evaluate the initiative?
2. Are you willing and able to commit the time, energy, and material resources necessary for the evaluation?
3. Can you live with disconfirmation?
4. Who will do the evaluation?
5. What do you want to assess?
6. How long do you expect your initiative to take to have a significant effect on students?
7. To what will you compare your process and outcome measures?

Source: Berkowitz, M.W. & CEP Assessment Committee. A Primer for Evaluating a Character Education Initiative. The Character Education Partnership. Used by permission.

Why Do You Want to Evaluate the Initiative?

The reason for an evaluation of the program should be clear with the program's stakeholders. Measurement ought to be conducted to make sure that the program is doing what it is supposed to be doing.

Are You Willing and Able to Commit the Time, Energy, and Material Resources Necessary for the Evaluation?

Seldom do athletic programs spend the time, energy, and resources necessary to appropriately evaluate their program. Fall season rolls into winter with very little time for thoughtful reflection. Most stakeholders believe that having a character-based athletic program is a good thing. However, there tends to be a lot more talk than action on this matter.

Can You Live with Disconfirmation?

Many athletic programs say that they're character-based. By making a valid and reliable assessment of your program, you declare what really is happening. To claim to be a character-based program warrants more than an advertisement on a banner in the school cafeteria, a core virtue written on a shingle above the locker room door, or a statement on a private school's brochure or Web site that suggests the school builds the character of its students. The stakeholder's character really shows if "the rubber meets the road" when the program is assessed.

Who Will Do the Evaluation?

Although athletic directors typically conduct staff and program evaluations, all stakeholder groups should be represented. Also the involvement of officials' organizations and perhaps the representation of other league schools will help make a more valid assessment. This will also take the onus of responsibility off the athletic director.

What Do You Want to Assess?

It is important for the evaluation team to be clear on what is being considered. If you are assessing the athletic program's mission, you should make sure that you are measuring the objectives of the program.

How Long Do You Expect Your Initiative to Take to Have a Significant Effect on Students?

Programs that claim they change behavior and character in limited periods of time usually have invested in a toxic dose of magical thinking. It takes time to develop lasting behavioral responses.

To What Will You Compare Your Process and Outcome Measures?

Marvin Berkowitz and the CEP Committee claim that "often we assume the process we intended is being implemented—but the assumption may not be warranted. It is important for an organization to know its approach to evaluating the program."

It is important to look at both process and outcome measures of a character-based athletic program—to make sure that the process and outcomes being measured are part of your program's goals. One way of evaluating the process is to use a formative assessment. For example, if an athletic program wants to assess coaching behavior, the aim of a formative evaluation is to assist coaches in reflecting on what they do and how they act with their teams. Lisa Lahey, of Harvard University's Graduate School of Education, suggests guidelines for this method of evaluation:

- Observe how a coach acts in relationship to the athletic program's core virtues.

- Establish criteria that describe observed actions in behavioral language. This must be fine-tuned—adjusted and narrowed to a specific language.

- Use either open or formal observation. An open observation concerns how the coach is viewed in respect to all the core values (virtues) in the mission. A formal observation may relate to a specific core value (virtue) such as patience or integrity.

Lahey notes that how often, how formal, and when the observations take place are important concerns.

A summative or outcome evaluation focuses on a coach's performance from an achievement or accountability criterion. It addresses all the coach's responsibilities and may include his or her won and lost records. If, however, we understand character to be enduring and not mutually exclusive from winning and losing, then records do not carry the heaviest weight in the character assessment piece.

Standardizing the Measurement of Virtue

Typical evaluations of athletic programs are subjective, which makes consensus difficult. Programs would be better served if they objectively measured virtue by attaching certain standards to certain behaviors. What is respect? What does it look like in our athletic program? How is courage displayed on and off the playing field? This gives the evaluator hard data that can be objectively measured. Some schools and organizations use objective measures such as yellow and red cards, ejections, and technical fouls to measure the character of their coaches. We suggest that, in addition, programs spend the time and energy to assess coaches based on the core virtues of the mission. The evaluation should include monitoring how coaches model behavior, conduct dialogue with their student-athletes, and carry out logical consequences for actions that do and do not reflect the core virtues of the mission.

Jeff Beedy's SportsPLUS program brings the measurement of virtue to a simple and effective level for coaches and athletes with the development of objective criteria called the "leader-detractor" scale. This method of assessment allows the evaluator to focus on the specific behavior and its relationship to the standards set in the team/program's mission. Beedy says, "With the help of the scales, behaviors and actions can be discussed with a child in more understandable ways. When both the coach and the child recognize where a behavior falls on the PLUS scale, the coach and child can then set goals for the child to move up the scale by changing specific behaviors." As you read the assessment criteria for each virtue, shown in Figure 7.4, note how each core virtue is broken down into objective standards.

One way of standardizing virtue is to clearly define each character habit in terms of what it looks like in action. For example, "sportsmanship" in The Montclair Kimberley Academy's mission can be objectively measured, and the measurement can be applied to any action taken by a coach, administrator, parent, student-athlete, or general spectator at a game.

Sportsmanship—We believe that winning is not just achieved on a scoreboard, but also requires the highest standards of conduct from every athlete, coach and spectator involved.

Figure 7.4. The PLUS Leader-to-Detractor Scale

TEAMWORK

Sports provide opportunities for players with different backgrounds and interests to relate to one another as members of the same team. Teamwork is an important life skill.

Levels of Teamwork

5.0   Understands role as a contributing team member plus models the value of teamwork.

4.0   Understands role as a member of team and seeks opportunities to display teamwork.

3.0   Understands role as a member of a team with common goals but displays little proactive teamwork.

2.0   Engages in teamwork only when directed and to promote self-interests.

1.0   Detracts from the team. No regard for teammates. "One person team," hogs the ball.

RESPECT

Respect is a fundamental value that, along with responsibility, forms the basis of the moral fabric for any family, team, or community. Respect for self and others requires that we treat all forms of life as inherently special. From respect stem many other virtues, such as compassion, courtesy, honesty, respect for authority, and respect for differences in ability, race, culture, and gender.

Levels of Respect

5.0   Communicates and displays through actions deep concern and caring for the person's worth as a human. Commits to enabling the other person's growth.

4.0   Communicates caring and concern for the other person. Makes others feel valued as individuals.

3.0   Expression of minimal acknowledgment, regard, or concern for the person's feelings, experience, or potential.

2.0   No thought for the feelings, experience, and potential of the other person.

1.0   Negative regard. Lack of respect, hurts other's feelings.

RESPONSIBILITY

Responsibility is the active side of respect and calls for acting upon one's moral values. Responsibility is the glue that holds a team, family, or community together. It is one thing to respect your teammate and it is another to take the responsibility to show that respect in tangible actions. Responsibility is also the moral extension of caring. It is the carrying out of our obligation to someone or to something (such as the team) greater than ourselves. A sense of responsibility to oneself, to a friend, to a coach, teacher, or parent, to a class, family, or team forms a base for our actions.

	Levels of Responsibility
5.0	Takes an active role in being accountable to the team plus actively models responsibility for others.
4.0	Understands role in situations plus seeks opportunities to be responsible.
3.0	Understands what it means to be responsible but takes no active role.
2.0	Assumes responsibility/accountability when confronted directly.
1.0	Avoids becoming responsible/accountable. "Here it comes, there I go."

Beedy, J. (1997). *Sports Plus. Developing Youth Sport Programs that Teach Positive Values.* Hamilton, MA: Project Adventure, pps. 41–45. Used by permission.

During a basketball playoff game at MKA, a fan in the stands shouted out as the opposing team's player was taking a free throw —unacceptable behavior in MKA's mission. As soon as the noise was made, both the school's athletic director and headmaster stood up from their seats on opposite ends of the gymnasium and converged in the direction of noise. Suddenly red-faced in embarrassment, an adolescent fan knew right away that he had made a big mistake. This behavior is not tolerated in MKA's gym.

MKA eventually lost the game. Ironically, when the winning team advanced to the next round, there was a major spectator disturbance that necessitated stoppage of the game for a period of time. When expectations are clear and supported, as they were in MKA's gym, the opportunities for quality performance, enjoyment, and satisfaction are mostly likely to be available. These same qualities are compromised when the expectations are not clear, as they were in the subsequent contest.

Rewarding Good Character—Acknowledgment or Mixed Message?

The act of rewarding individuals, teams, and/or programs for displaying good character is controversial. Some may view this as acknowledging uncommon acts of good "sportsmanship"—things that seem to be above and beyond the call of duty. Rewards are also used as reinforcement or motivation for others to act in the same manner. That, on the surface, is sound thinking. However, shouldn't it be an expectation of programs that participants follow the mission statement regardless of the motivation to earn a "good sport certificate"? Many people suggest that sportsmanship awards should be a reflection of the program's mission. Unfortunately, some of the criteria for this reward may not necessarily reflect the program's mission.

When athletic programs earn a sportsmanship award one year and are censured by the league or state association the next for violations of the same sportsmanship code, then a red flag ought to be raised. Although the personnel of teams changes from year to year, with seniors graduating and freshmen entering the athletic program, programs that are founded on good character, ideally, don't run the gamut from being recipients of the award one year to being sanctioned soon after. There ought to be a common thread running within the athletic program that continually refers back to the core virtues aspired to in the program. In rebuttal, a coach or athletic director may say that an isolated incident can prompt the censuring. This must be acknowledged. However, athletic programs that are clear and consistent in their mission tend to achieve a sense of balance that helps to safeguard against inappropriate actions.

Walking the Talk

When core virtues are acted on by adult mentors and expected of the student-athletes, it gives the athletes a greater opportunity to apply these virtues to their individual and team performances. It is often overlooked that a person's character is not mutually exclusive from winning and losing. In fact, virtuous behavior can and does influence performance in a positive way. Good coaches who espouse the core virtues of the program can blend them into their daily practices in the teaching of sport specific skills and habits.

(8)

Walking the Talk II—
Character Links to Performance

*The lessons are straightforward: There is no path to
excellence at anything except the deliberate, purposeful
formation of daily habits that make the specific form of
excellence possible. There are no shortcuts, and mere
talent is not enough.*
   Edwin J. Delattre—*Sport: A Crucible of Aspiration*

*At a recent Character and Sport Initiative conference, Peter Greer, the
headmaster of The Montclair Kimberley Academy, narrated a compelling
story about a young boy's Little League experience. The boy was not
known for being a good hitter. In fact, he didn't swing the bat at all and
would consequently be called out on strikes every time he came to home
plate. It was agonizing for his mother and father to listen to angry parents saying awful things about their wonderful son—all because he could-
n't hit the ball. At the end of the season, the team was playing in an
important game and the boy came to the plate in a critical situation with
teammates on base and the team behind by a couple of runs. True to
form, the bat didn't leave his shoulder for three pitches. After the game,
the dejected son said to his proud and caring father: "Dad, I really wish
I could hit." The father was elated and said, "Yes. I will find you the best
help available. We will work on it every day. We will make you a hitter."
His son's reply was, "But, Dad, I don't want to work at it. I just want to
hit." He had not yet learned the difference between wishing and willing.
Dr. Greer affirms that we must will good habits, we must will improved
skills—we just cannot wish them to happen.*

Performance Excellence—Wishing and Willing

An athlete who has developed a strong character can call on a foundation of well-formed habits in aspiring to achieve true excellence. The competition of the sport arena, together with a personal goal to optimize performance, challenges the athlete to continuously stretch his or her abilities through deliberate practice—focused and effortful rehearsal. Deliberate practice requires a good degree of patience and perseverance. More often than not, the initial process of improvement, guided by practice, requires that athletes be willing to make choices different from what they 'feel like doing" in the moment.

Athletes that are committed to improving their performance quickly learn that one of the most significant sources of both difficulty and joy comes from the ability to rise to the challenge —they don't back down from heightened levels of lactic acid build-up or momentary lapses in motivation. The ability to stretch beyond one's perceived ability or desire and to continue is contingent on asking, "What is the *right* action—what needs to be done *at this time* to improve performance—right now?" This allows the miler to push a little harder on the last lap, the football player to extend in the weight room, and the injured athlete to remain faithful to the demands of physical therapy so that rehabilitation will be effective. And with this effort also comes the joy and satisfaction of sport. When the body and mind adapt to higher demands, the adaptation leads, inexorably, to a heightened sense of engagement and enjoyment, a "dog-with-a-bone" type of satisfaction.

The Flow State

Michaeli Csikszentmihalyi's model of flow, the ability to be engaged in and enjoy the process of any endeavor, clearly illustrates the importance of an athlete's willingness to meet challenges that are marginally equal to or above his or her current skill level (see Figure 8.1). If the athlete's skill level is higher than the challenge, boredom sets in. In contrast, when the athlete's skill level is relatively lower than the challenge, anxiety enters the equation. Only when challenge meets skill can the individual be fully engaged in and enjoy the endeavor for the sheer sake of participation. When enjoyment is paired with enhanced sport performance, it is impossible for the relationship between challenge and skill to remain stagnant.

Csikszentmihalyi describes flow as a dynamic process of differentiation and integration. Differentiation occurs when athletes stretch themselves, when the demand is slightly beyond their current abilities. Integration results when the skill/ability meets the new challenge. When this happens, challenge meets skills with a focused and pr ent effort. This results in greater engagement, enjoyment, and performance.

FIGURE 8.1 The Csikszentmihalyi Flow Model

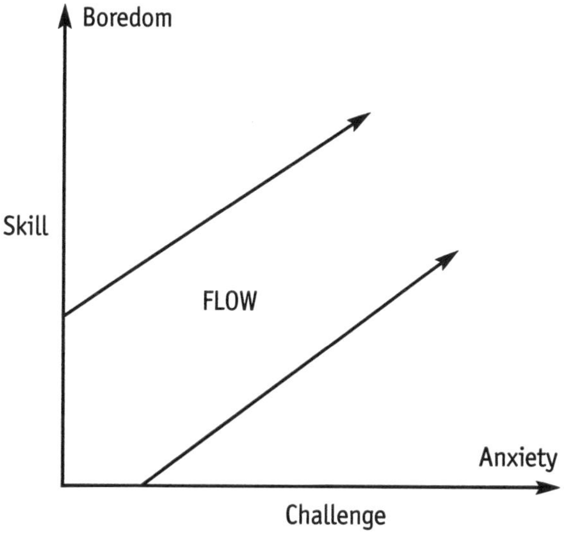

It is important for coaches to understand the flow model, in that it reinforces the necessity for athletes to be willing to push beyond what they feel like doing. When experiencing the flow state, the athlete is fully enjoying the process and wants to continue participation. Cindy Adams, a former elite figure skater, and a sport psychologist who has worked with Olympic and professional athletes, vividly recalls a flow experience in her skating career.

I remember one night at the Broadmoor in Colorado Springs. There were two rinks and we would skate at 10 or 11 at night to 3 or 4 in the morning. Those were our training hours. I was in the big rink and decided to go to the little rink. Then there was the unbelievable moment. I remember going in and saying goodnight to others as they left. And I was alone. I had a mirror, my own little rink (the curling rink), and my music box. I put on my music—not the regular dance music—and I was in front of the mirror, doing positions. I remember how much I loved being on the ice at that moment. I stopped for a moment and thought: "You know, if you just keep practicing, just keep moving, this will all pay off one day." I remember thinking that I want to be the last one on the ice, because I know that if I work really, really hard and I believe in this, and I am dedicated to what I am doing right now, good things will happen. I remember all of those thoughts as I just enjoyed the music, all by myself, as my partner had gone home, too. It was a total absence of anyone, and a total enjoyment of everything.

Unfortunately, the flow state is not the dominant experience in sport. During the more difficult differentiation moments, when the challenge is slightly beyond their comfort level and flow states, some athletes simply do not have the capability needed to rise to the occasion. Others are able to draw on the habits of good character they have previously formed. This makes it much easier to make the right choices in the moment—not what they feel like doing, but what needs to be done!

Many athletes are unaware that these character traits are summoned to action at the critical moments in a practice or a game. They remark that they just did what they needed to do, a result of ritual and deliberate practice. It is important to note that many athletes and coaches do not think about this process much, since deliberate practice may be second nature. The work ethic has been engraved in such a way that undertaking the task is a measure of their character—integrity, self-discipline, and perseverance.

Factors of Skilled Performance

Although some people may be born with exceptional athletic ability, a combination of many factors contributes to developing a skilled experience. Leonard Zaichkowsky, a leading sport psychologist with college and professional teams, and Jerry Larson, the head of school at Cheshire Academy, break performance down into six primary factors that support the development of a skilled performance (see Figure 8.2). These include fitness, physical endowments, motor skills, cognitive understanding, sport skill, and psychological factors. Most of these factors, beyond obvious constraints such as height, can be enhanced through both physical and mental practice.

First, successful performers need to be fit. This factor can be further divided into cardiorespiratory endurance, muscular strength and endurance, and flexibility. Second, physical endowments, such as physique, weight, height, and vision, have important implications. Third, cognitive understanding of time and space—how one reads and reacts to situations—influences performance. Fourth, motor skills, including speed, reaction time, agility, and coordination, are critical. Fifth, athletes need to develop their sport-specific skills if they expect to attain their athletic goals. Finally, numerous psychological components contribute to performance. These encompass formation of traits such as commitment, desire to excel, desire to win, self-confidence, emotional stability, and self-control.

Figure 8.2 Factors Influencing Skilled Performance

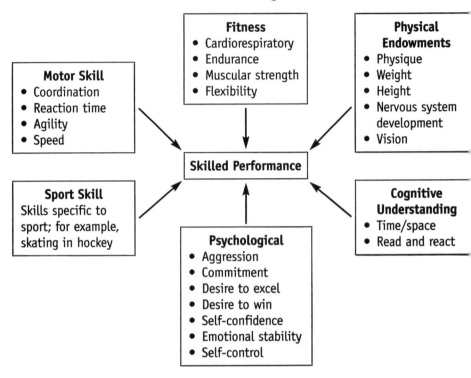

Fitness
- Cardiorespiratory
- Endurance
- Muscular strength
- Flexibility

Physical Endowments
- Physique
- Weight
- Height
- Nervous system development
- Vision

Motor Skill
- Coordination
- Reaction time
- Agility
- Speed

Skilled Performance

Sport Skill
Skills specific to sport; for example, skating in hockey

Psychological
- Aggression
- Commitment
- Desire to excel
- Desire to win
- Self-confidence
- Emotional stability
- Self-control

Cognitive Understanding
- Time/space
- Read and react

What separates successful performers from others is the ability to make the most of what they *can* control in their aspirations for optimal performance. This doesn't mean that anyone can become an elite athlete. But it does mean that athletes can strive to perform to the best of their ability levels—aspiring to excellence as individuals and as members of a team. Malcolm Gladwell's August 1999 article in *The New Yorker,* "The Physical Genius," supports these assumptions. The "physical genius" wills performance, rather than wishes it. Deliberate practice requires concentration and doing what needs to be done. This provides the athlete with the knowledge of what to do at the right moment on the playing field.

What sets physical geniuses apart from other people, then, is not merely being able to do something but

*knowing what to do—their capacity to pick up on
subtle patterns that others generally miss. This is
what we mean when we say that great athletes have
a "feel" for the game, or that they "see" the court or
the field or the ice in a special way. If you think of
physical genius as a pyramid, with, at the bottom,
the raw components of coordination, and, above that,
the practice that perfects those particular movements,
then this faculty of imagination is the top layer. This
is what separates physical genius from those who are
merely very good.*

Gladwell's illustration suggests that the fruits of success
that result from deliberate practice by the "physical genius" are
rooted in the virtues of integrity, self-discipline, patience, and
perseverance. The "physical genius" wills performance, rather
than wishes it.

Character and Performance

Athletes who are able to perform in a flow state tend to maintain
a high level of concentration and attention, i.e., a state character-
ized by the absence of distraction. *Distraction* is a key word, since
the goal of performing well is to minimize anything that takes the
athlete's mind away from the task at hand. Generally, when people are doing something well they are experiencing very low levels
of distraction. We know from research that when distraction goes
up, performance goes down—a correlation that applies to sport,
music, test taking, and numerous other activities.

The relationship works the other way as well. When distraction goes down, performance goes up. The absence of distraction
may not be the main reason an athlete performs well—other factors can influence performance. However, athletes who are fully
attentive to the task at hand will probably perform to their given
capabilities. When this is combined with minimal distraction,
they can have a pretty good outing.

There are various types of distraction, and these could be categorized into four major areas: physical, mental, social, emotional. The physical areas include low energy level, injury, and hunger. The mental category might include, for example, an athlete's uncertainty regarding his or her assignment. The social category includes such distractions as an athlete's feeling that she doesn't fit in as a member of the team or experiencing a low comfort level when she is with the coaching staff. Finally, there are emotional distractions, such as a fight with a boyfriend or girlfriend, or with Mom and Dad, prior to a contest. This category also includes situations that may be more serious, requiring professional attention. (Keep in mind that these categories often overlap).

Consider a simple illustration by Mark Boyea. The top set of bars in Figures 8.3 represent the capacity for concentration that accompanies an athletic performance for an elite, average and novice athlete. When the athlete has been injured, awareness and concentration tend to focus on the injury. This distraction eats away a bit at the open space within the lower set of bars. The more that such distractions are allowed to enter the bar, the smaller the open space within the bar gets. The athlete has less capacity to focus on the task, and the level of performance decreases.

Each athlete has a certain amount of available space. The size of the bar will vary from person to person, depending on such factors as motor skills, sport skills, cognitive understanding, fitness level, physical endowments and psychological skills. Elite athletes have larger bars. If they become slightly distracted, they can probably still perform pretty well. Other athletes, specifically high school athletes and relatively inexperienced coaches, generally have much smaller bars. They can stand only a certain amount of distraction. The higher the level of innate ability and training, the larger the bar is. The implication for coaching is this: You have to know where your people are to know how much and what kinds of distraction they can withstand, and still perform well.

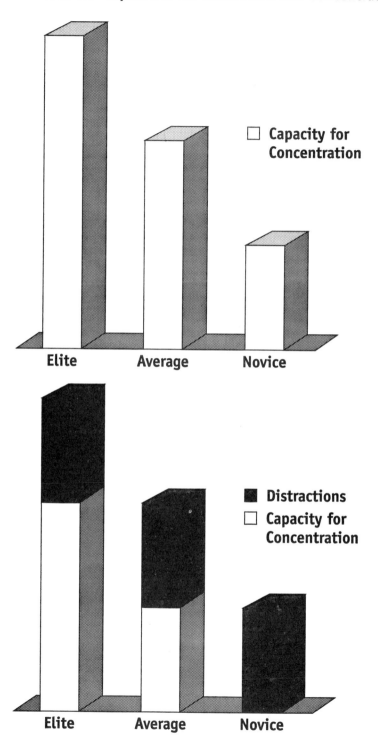

FIGURE 8.3 Capacities for Distraction and Concentration

Elite   Average   Novice

☐ Capacity for Concentration

■ Distractions
☐ Capacity for Concentration

Elite   Average   Novice

The concepts of attention and distraction relate to character in many ways. Trust is a good example. An individual's ability to trust the person at the next level above them is critical. This involves the athlete-to-coach relationship as well as the coach-to-athletic director relationship, and the athletic director-to-principal (or head of school) relationship. When things get tight on the field, even a small amount of doubt can take some of the space in the bar away. The more distracted an athlete or coach may be, the greater likelihood of making a bad decision. It is important for the athletic director, principal (or head of school), and coach that the people who report to them can trust them. If not, the coach or administrator has played a part in creating distraction and taken away from the opportunity for success.

Trust also applies to action on the field. When an athlete is not sure about the preparation of a fellow teammate, doubt begins to creep in. This may distract the athlete at a critical time and diminish the likelihood of the team performing at its best.

The same principle applies in the case of caring. Caring is synonymous with "mattering," with the sense that other people are important and that we should be concerned with their well being. Coaches and other stakeholders not only need to trust the people they work with, they also need to care about those people —to be truly concerned with athletes' welfare. Caring is not the same as liking. Coaches can be demanding, but still show that they are concerned about the athlete. Adult mentors can't fake a caring attitude; young athletes can smell phony behavior a mile away. They know if a coach is not authentic and genuine. Athletic directors ought to be aware of this when they recruit new staff members. The advice is this: If you want your program to reach its potential, you need to be concerned about hiring adult mentors who demonstrate genuine concern for the welfare of the athlete.

However, it should be noted that there are successful coaches who are not "good" people. They are the minority, but

they do exist. It is important to ur
are not talented enough that the⌐
through having a deficient char⌐
character will influence perfor⌐
lenge to coaches, cited in Ch⌐
that good that you can get ⌐
your own distractions through de⌐
playing for you and I can't trust you, ⌐ ⌐
traction. In a tight game, mistrust creates a ⌐
a moment of hesitation in carrying out your directⁱ⌐
coach." The potential is there! Therefore, coaches can't a⌐
be sloppy. Do you want to take the risk? The bottom line is tha⌐
character will influence performance.

Applying Mental Skills to Promote Right Action and Improve Performance

The mental aspect of the athlete's training regime, reinforced
by the formation of good character habits, can be an invaluable
component for optimizing performance. In this regard, the techniques known as "mental skills training" provide an effective,
structured way to train an athlete's mind to improve performance. With the use of psychological skills, athletes improve both
their mental and physical responses in several important ways.
Specifically, the training enhances concentration, improves technical skills, builds effective mechanisms for coping with sport
stress (performance anxiety), and aids in control of emotional
responses.

Several common threads run throughout the sport psychology
literature, and these themes point to mental training skills that
transcend sport domains. They include developing competitive
plans, setting daily training goals, establishing game simulations
in practice, building high confidence (developing sport-specific
self-efficacy), maintaining task-oriented positive thoughts,
adjusting and coping with the unexpected, and overcoming
obstacles by planning.

...ills can be grouped into four general categories:
...ting, (2) visualization, (3) self-talk, and (4) arousal
...—the conscious control of mind and body responses in
...rt to achieve optimal performance. The following discus-
...ooks at how each of these mental skills, when reinforced
...good character habits, can contribute to improved perform-
...ce. The result is behavior that supports right action, which
reflects the drive for optimizing performance, versus behaviors
that are reflective of the participant's momentary desires.

Goal Setting

A goal is an objective, standard, or aim of some action. It is
important to distinguish between subjective and objective goals,
in that goal setting is most effective when the athlete establishes
clear and consistent aims. Subjective goals are based on individual judgment or discretion, thereby making them difficult to
measure. Often subjective goals are represented by such outcomes
as "having fun" or "doing one's best."

Although these outcomes are desirable, it is more effective to
also establish objective and measurable goals, such as attaining a
specific standard of proficiency on a task in a specified time period.
Examples of objective goals include a miler's effort to improve his or
her time from four minutes and ten seconds to four minutes, or a
basketball player's improving his or her free throw percentage from
65 percent to 75 percent over a three-month period. Also, it is more
effective to set personal performance goals rather than outcome
goals based on comparisons with other athletes.

The acronym SMART provides a useful tool for developing a
goal-setting strategy. The first principle, represented by the letter
"S," underscores the importance of setting *specific* goals. The athlete must clarify what he or she is committed to achieving. For
example, an athlete who states that she wants to "decrease her
200 meter swim by one second" has a specific goal; the swimmer
who just wants to "get better" does not. The clearer the goal, the

better the chance the athlete will develop a strategy leading to achieving the goal.

Second, the goal needs to be *measurable*. The previous example illustrates measurability. Measuring "getting better" is a subjective process, whereas "decreasing time by one second" is objective.

Third, the goals must be *adjustable*. Once a goal is set, particularly a long-term goal, the athlete must be willing to adjust what he or she originally committed to achieving. For example, the athlete may be slowed down by injury, over-training, or some other factor as he or she comes closer to achieving the goal.

The fourth principle is having *realistic* goals—such as short-term daily, weekly, and monthly goals. Setting goals that are too lofty invites disappointment. While aspiring and dreaming long into the future can be inspirational, it is important that the athlete or team can be successful with short-term goals.

Finally, the fifth principle underscores the importance of setting *time-sensitive* goals. This process requires a commitment to declaring when the goal will be achieved. There is a distinct difference, for example, between a football player's statement that he will increase his bench press by 10 percent, and the commitment to increasing his one-rep maximum by 10 percent at the end of a three-month period. Setting a time limit imposes a sense of urgency for the athlete to create an appropriate strategy with a realistic timeline. In a recent interview, one world champion athlete commented on the importance of daily goals. She explained that the process involves

> *continually setting goals for yourself, meeting them.*
> *And then you have to start all over again. But that is*
> *how you have to get through it. If you look at the over-*
> *all picture, there is no way, it seems insurmountable.*
> *You know, if I had ever at the beginning of last year*
> *thought, my goal is to win a gold medal at the world*

championships, I never would have. I never thought about that until at the world championships . . . It was just like all these little steps.

The interview puts a spotlight on the influence goal setting can have on enhanced performance. The ability to be patient and focus on the little steps empowered this athlete to achieve a performance level in sport beyond her imagination.

Terry Orlick, a world-renowned sport psychologist, has worked with athletes at all levels over the past thirty years. Orlick claims that the athlete must first have goal clarity and a specific knowledge of what he or she would like to achieve. Second, goal setting can not be successful unless the athlete is willing to commit to achieving the goal. The foundation for this commitment is built on integrity and courage. Commitment requires that the athlete's actions are consistent when striving toward a goal regardless of the barriers. Remaining committed to a goal often requires courage, willfully acting with patience and perseverance. Third, the athlete must have a strong belief in his or her abilities. Fourth, the athlete must have some form of social support. Finally, the athlete must accept the possibility of failure. Without this acceptance there tends to be a lot of wasted energy and focus on worrying about whether or not they will be successful.

Visualization/Imagery

Clearly, many coaches and athletes have experienced a time in their sport experience when everything seemed to be perfect— just the right amount of arousal, the right amount of muscle tension, and the right amount of alertness. For athletes to optimize their chances of performing well, it is important to be able to recapture those moments using visual (sight), auditory (hearing), and kinesthetic (touch and feel) memory. This reflection allows the athlete to sense what the optimal situation looked like, sounded like, and felt like. Performance imagery is about reliving that powerful moment, recapturing and replaying it. And for those who have yet to have had such experiences, imagery can be used to create experiences that the athlete strives to achieve.

Imagery is the process of constructing mental pictures, either real or imagined. It is a means of communication between the mind, body, and spirit. We use imagery all the time, whether we realize it or not. For example, the smell of the fresh cut grass on the playing field, the distinctive color of the opposing team's uniforms, the cutting sound of skates as they glide over freshly made ice—these and other images remind athletes and coaches of a specific time and place when they performed either well or poorly. Unfortunately, it is easy for some coaches and athletes to imagine negative events, and in a self-fulfilling prophecy, actually play out the poor performance, time after time.

We once conducted a limited study of performance anxiety and imagery with a group of female college gymnasts. We measured their heart rate, skin temperature, blood volume, and muscle tension as they watched a videotape of a gymnast falling off the balance beam. We were surprised to see the consistency of their physical reactions to the fall. Each subject expressed a pained facial expression and an overall body tension. After watching the videotape, each subject mentioned that she tended to construct negative images and lose her balance more frequently.

Conversely, by visualizing good action, by seeing ourselves coaching well and playing well, we fill our minds with healthy, constructive thoughts. Imagery also helps us learn to focus on the immediate, ultimately eliminating the dissonance of the environment. For some coaches and athletes, it takes a great effort to deliberately practice sport-related imagery.

Self-Talk

Self-talk is simply defined as intrapersonal dialogue, essentially any thoughts or statements coaches and athletes make to themselves. Sport psychologist Lew Hardy and his fellow researchers claim that we are often not aware of the thoughts that directly influence our emotions and subsequent behaviors. With self-talk training, the athlete can learn to enhance many facets of performance such as skill acquisition, breaking bad habits, initiating or motivating action, and sustaining effort. At the core, self-talk training supports athletes in interpreting their reality in an alternate way, such that enhanced performance is possible. One way of changing perspectives is to "reframe" one's experience. Steven Ungerleider, in his book *Mental Training for Peak Performance*, provides an example of a champion athlete who is able to reframe his sport experience:

> *Bruce Jenner used to interpret increased heartbeat, muscle tremor, rapid breathing, increased sweating and a need to urinate just before the decathlon as a sign that he was nervous, excessively aroused and wasn't going to do well. These thoughts inevitably led to a self-fulfilling prophecy. Over time, he reframed those feelings and thoughts and told himself that he was ready, prepared both physically and psychologically and that those symptoms were a sign of readiness and positive signals to compete. The results? An Olympic gold in the decathlon in 1976.*

This is a dramatic example of the power of reframing one's thoughts. However, it must be noted that Bruce Jenner's ability to enhance performance occurred over a period of time and that the mental training was paired with intense physical training. Psychological skills in general are useful only if they are practiced over time, just as consistent, effortful physical practice is required for improving physical performance.

Albert Bandura, a professor at Stanford University and a pioneer in social learning theory, discusses the power of cognitive restructuring, another way of changing one's self-talk to improve athletic performance. Bandura notes that when the athlete is focused on negative thoughts, these thoughts interfere with the athlete's ability to focus on the task at hand in a way that would allow the athlete to optimize performance. He claims that "The cognitive control task is to stop rumination over a mistake or failure, which is likely to breed only further mistakes. [E]fforts to control unwanted thoughts by suppressing them can backfire because such attempts only draw attention to them or create reminders of them. People can better rid themselves of disruptive thinking by concentrating their attention on the task at hand and generating helpful thinking." Cognitive restructuring, focusing on one's performance in the moment, allows the athlete to optimize performance.

The table, below, provides examples of how the athlete can use self-talk to improve in each of four challenge areas by using cognitive restructuring/reframing.

TABLE 8.1 REFRAMING NEGATIVE SELF-TALK			
Challenge	Negative Self-Talk	Cognitive Restructuring/ Re-framing	Character Habit
Skill Acquisition	"I'm a terrible technician."	"I will practice an extra hour each day to improve my technique."	Moderation and Balance Courage
Breaking Bad Habits	"I can't catch the ball."	"eyes on the ball" "I can catch."	Courage Care and Compassion
Initiating or Motivating Action	"I just don't want to go to practice today."	"I am a team player. I matter to my team. If I don't go, they can't play."	Care and Compassion Justice Integrity
Sustaining Effort	"I am too tired. I just can't do it."	"I have trained hard. I can and will do my best."	Integrity Courage

When coaches and athletes become aware of their self-talk within the formal structure of sport, they then can begin the work of redirecting or reinterpreting the negative or destructive thoughts and thought patterns. As the table illustrates, enhancing one's self-talk is often aligned and consistent with the formation of good character habits, and both self-talk and character ultimately enhance the athlete's ability to perform in sport. It must be noted that, as with the other psychological skills, changing one's self-talk must be consistently practiced over time. The advice to athletes is this: Becoming aware of your thoughts is a powerful first step. However, it is imperative that you practice change. Change will not happen simply because you are aware of your self-talk.

Changing an athlete's self-talk to enhance performance requires both courage and integrity on the part of the athlete, as well as care and compassion from the coach or mentor. The athlete must be willing to accept moments when he or she is overwhelmed with negative or destructive thoughts and is unable to effectively respond. However, with integrity the athlete can stay the course and ultimately achieve changed cognitive responses, which ultimately will enhance performance.

Performance Arousal

Yuri Hanin, a professor at the Research Institute for Olympic Sports in Jyväskylä, Finland, has conducted extensive research in the area of performance arousal. The results show that sometimes coaches and athletes are too uptight, too psyched up for a contest—meaning that they are over-aroused. In extreme over-arousal, the physiological signs include increased heart rate, racing thoughts, profuse sweating, and tense muscles which is related to relatively poor performance. There are other times when coaches and athletes are under-aroused—meaning they are in a lethargic, "I don't care" state of mind and performance is again adversely affected.

FIGURE 8.4 Zones of Optimal Performance

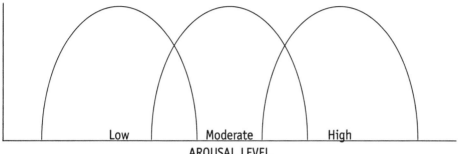

Low · Moderate · High
AROUSAL LEVEL

This model is a combination of two well-respected sport psychology arousal-performance models; the Inverted-U Hypothesis (Yerkes-Dodson) and Hanon's Individual Zones of Optimal Functioning Model.

The model in Figure 8.4 illustrates how athletes respond to arousal differently. For some athletes, it is best to approach competition when feeling calm and relaxed. For others, they need to be a little more excited. And, at the other end of the continuum, the remaining athletes do best when they are highly charged. This type of athlete benefits most from the "pep-talk" prior to the game.

For each type of athlete, performance is optimized at low, medium or high levels of arousal, and this continuum of arousal levels will differentially influence performance. For all types of athletes, at their lower end of the continuum, when under aroused, performance tends to be poorer. As arousal is increased, performance tends to increase. There is a bandwidth in the middle that we call the optimal point of arousal—in essence, a zone of excellence. This is where the athlete can enter a flow state, maintaining the right amount of arousal to be at his or her best. That is the state where the athlete wants to be.

Performance goes up as arousal goes up—to a certain degree. As we increase arousal past this point, performance will tend to decrease, i.e., performance goes down as arousal continues to increase. In dealing with athletes, the advice is this: If you sense that your level of arousal is low, then you need to do something to get yourself up; and if you are too aroused, slow the system down.

Increasing Performance Arousal

When athletes realize that their arousal level is down, they can respond by voluntarily increasing the rate of breathing, by exercising and getting the blood flowing and muscle activity going. Also, imaging the perfect state of arousal—the flow state—can help increase readiness, and self-talk may help in encouraging a readiness state. Coaches and athletes can use phrases such as "be alert," "be active," and "pumped up."

Decreasing Performance Arousal

When performance in an important game is at stake, coaches and parents should remember that some athletes will actually not perform well when over-aroused. Sometimes overzealous pep talks or aggressive fans can throw players off their games, and that is typically when physical injuries happen. When athletes get too anxious, their minds race too much, their bodies sweat excessively, and heart rates are accelerated. To bring all this down into that optimal zone, the athlete needs to reverse strategy for increasing arousal.

One strategy to decrease performance arousal is to ask players to breath more slowly—to use slow, deep diaphragmatic breathing. This slows down the heart rate, slows down the amount of sweat given off, and releases muscle tension. A body scan of the important muscles of the arms and legs may be helpful to make sure they are in the optimal zone. Also, athletes can use progressive muscle relaxation by voluntarily tensing and relaxing muscles. First, an individual tenses certain muscles in the body, becoming aware of how the tension feels, and then relaxes the muscles, releasing the tension. The procedure enables the athlete to become more aware of skeletal muscle action, the same action used in the sport, and eventually develop more voluntary control—not too tight, not too relaxed. When athletes deliberately practice these activities, they become more aware of what it feels like to be in the optimal zone.

Gary Hamill, a tennis coach and sport psychology consultant, investigated the zone of excellence with elite amateur tennis players. Each player in the study wore a heart rate monitor strapped around the chest. The monitor fed data on heart rate to a computer chip in the watch on the player's hand, where it was stored. A researcher in the stands observed and recorded the play of the athlete. After the match, the players' heart rate data were downloaded onto a computer and compared with the historical information recorded on video. Although there was some variability from individual to individual, the results showed that many of the players in the study had heart rates that were significantly consistent when they played well, and were out of this zone when they were not playing their best. This is a wonderful teaching tool to help athletes estimate what their optimal heart rate zone is and make appropriate adaptations of their arousal level. It is important for athletes and coaches to be able to moderate arousal levels. Heart rate is just one physiological measure of arousal level, there are many other types of feedback that athletes can call upon.

Process to Product

Performance excellence is a direct result of the process, the "means" by which an outcome is achieved. Coaches and athletes who possess good character have a greater opportunity to engage in the deliberate practice necessary to perform well. They have formed the habits of self-discipline, patience, and perseverance essential to master the mental skills that provide for skilled performance. All stakeholders in a sport program ought to carefully consider this principle, for the well being of both the athlete and others participating. Peter Greer's advice rings true: "We must will and put into action good habits, we must will improved skills—we cannot wish them to happen." The desire to succeed in the pursuit of excellence is based on this principle.

9

Next Steps—Expanding the Influence of Good Character in Sport

Having the skills today is a small part of the whole. Being committed to using them consistently tomorrow is the crux of it . . . Habit, obviously, relates to disposition. I have to want to apply these skills. Therefore, I must be convinced of their utility and reasonableness.   *Theodore Sizer—Horace's School*

For some coaches, making the commitment to develop and maintain a character-based athletic program is a difficult challenge. Although most coaches have good intentions and truly believe that "character matters" in the sport experience, such intentions and beliefs may not be enough. They must also know what virtue *looks like* when it comes alive on the field. They must understand that virtue is about developing habits of right action so that they become second nature. It is about behavior, and for some, it is about learning to *change* behavior.

People learn to change their behavior in different ways. There are no simple "just add water" methods for teaching coaches, athletic directors, athletes, parents and other program stakeholders how to be more virtuous—how to be more "sportsmanlike." Change in behavior can happen only when people make serious and enduring efforts. Jeff Beedy's book, *Sports Plus*, addresses the importance of understanding the different ways that people learn. Basing his insights on learning theory, Beedy emphasizes three activities that help bring virtue to life in sports: modeling, dialogue, and consequences. To apply this theory, we need only ask a series of pointed questions. If, for example, we believe that an athletic program is about trust and fairness, we can ask:

- What do trust and fairness look like when they are *modeled* by coaches and players? How does this behavior look in the performance of individual players and the collective team?

- What are the characteristics of *dialogue* or conversation that focuses on trust and fairness?

- And what are the *consequences* for a team or individual player when the coach has broken trust with reference to, say, an understanding that all players will participate?

Better yet, let's reframe that last question so that it has a positive spin: What are the consequences for a team or player when all involved consistently trust each other? The answer is simple—greater enjoyment and satisfaction, and possibly improved performance. We learn by knowing, by valuing, and by acting. There is no substitute for developing and reinforcing the "second nature habits" of good character.

The Challenge of Change—Staying the Course

It's no easy task to change an individual's or an organization's behavior. Although people value the sport experience for different reasons, we must never lose sight of the common denominator—that sport is primarily for the benefit of the participants. For those who are on board and are spreading the good word about "character matters in sport," it is important to be patient and stay the course.

James Prochaska and Carlo DiClemente are pioneer researchers in the area of health behavior change. Although their long-term research addresses health behaviors, we can readily adapt their Transtheoretical Model to illustrate the complexity of undertaking change in athletic organizations. Based on almost two decades of research on certain health behaviors, they claim that people go through predictable stages in the change process: pre-contemplation, contemplation, preparation, action, and mainte-nance. The model has a great number of helpful implications. Consider, for example, the frustration we often feel when an indi-vidual seems to lack motivation for change, or when that person's progress is slow. Prochaska and DiClemente's model assures us that people may actually have begun to change, even when there is no outward sign of change.

Let's take a close look at each of the stages, along with some suggestions for supporting change during that stage.

First, many people do not believe they need to do business differently when it comes to proper behavior on the athletic field. They have grown up with a win-at-all-costs, take-no-prisoners mentality regarding how sport should be played and coached, and they may have given little thought to seeing sport through a different lens. If so, they are in the **pre-contemplation** stage of change.

It is appropriate to be generous in trying to understand these folks. However, it would be misguided to condone some of the mixed messages they send to their young athletes. One way of helping people to begin to think about making a change is to provide them with information that "makes sense" to them and that raises consciousness on important issues. Certainly, events in the media spotlight, such as the story of the parent of a youth hockey player who allegedly beat his son's coach to death, can be a consciousness raiser. Also, statistics on the alarming drop out rate in youth sports may motivate someone to enter into an "internal conversation"—to begin to **contemplate** about what matters most in sport.

When people have sufficiently understood the need to act differently as coaches—to provide a healthier performance-conducive environment for the athletes—they can then **prepare** for the change. Preparing for change may involve making sure the mission of the team and athletic program is clear and consistent, and that the core virtues of the program are clearly defined and understood by all the program stakeholders—coaches, athletes, athletic director, parents, and others.

Preparation leads to action. **Action** is about what "good character" looks like on and off the field. The action consists of coaches, athletes, and parents exhibiting trust, courage, and moderation through their behavior.

Maintaining character-based athletic programs requires constant oversight, with adult mentors consistently "checking and balancing" the process. It is important to re-emphasize that athletic programs do not fall apart—they fray. The program's leaders subtly lose sight of their mission; they begin to allow little things to slip, such as lack of consequences for inappropriate fan behavior, players being late for practice, or athletes acting selfishly on the field. Programs should be frequently evaluated. The stakeholders should be asked to answer the important questions posed earlier in this book: Why are we doing what we are doing? Are we doing what we say we are doing? Are we making a difference with the athletes we serve?

When we know, value, and act on these questions, we take the influence of sport on character formation seriously. We show that character and sport matter. Therefore, it might be helpful to review and reinforce the five essential points formulated in the Introduction.

1. Personal History

Past sport experiences have a strong influence on how parents and coaches teach and coach their children/athletes. Adults must take time to reflect thoughtfully on their own experiences in order to understand the "why" of their values and behavior.

2. Walking the Talk

Modeling good behavior—to lead by deed—is a critical influence on young people's character development. By experiencing their coaches, parents, and mentors "walking the talk," young athletes will see that the commitment to ideals is genuine.

3. Partnership

There must be an ongoing partnership among school administrators, parents, and coaches regarding the character development of athletes. While parents are the prime character educators, all adults associated with the athletic program must embody and reflect the moral authority invested in them.

4. Accepting Responsibility

All those who work with young people must work to identify opportunities for positive modeling and growth. They also should work to create and identify the responsibilities they have to develop the athlete's character.

5. Evaluation

Those responsible for the athletic program need to stress the importance of the evaluation of these activities. Changing habits, developing and reinforcing good behavior, establishing standards of right and wrong action—all this takes time. Those who are serious about doing well by young people must be willing to measure the reality of their progress against their best intentions.

Coaching as Service—Coaching as Privilege

Lou Nanni, the executive assistant to the president of the University of Notre Dame, suggests that being a leader means, first of all, to serve—to care for the needs and wants of those in your charge. He also claims that having the opportunity to serve young people is a privilege. Whatever the circumstances that bring adults to coach, it is important that they continue to evaluate themselves by asking the important questions.

If the answers to those questions lead to the conclusion that, indeed, our purpose is to serve (a conclusion that seems unavoidable), then we must be faithful to our service. We share the wonderful opportunity—and the privilege—of having a profound influence on young people.

References

Introduction

p. x   Haywood Hale Broun's famous quote can be found in James Michner's *Sports in America* (New York: Random House, 1976).

p. xviii The advertisement for Deloitte Consulting, Inc., was seen in the Canadian Airlines in-flight magazine, September 1999.

Chapter 1

p. 8   Drew A. Hyland teaches the philosophy of sport at Trinity College. He is the author of *Philosophy of Sport,* Paragon Issues on Philosophy Series (St. Paul, MN: Paragon House, 1990).

p. 10   Drew A. Hyland, "Opponents, Contestants, and Competitors: The Dialectic of Sport," *Journal of the Philosophy of Sport,* Vol. 11 (1985), pp. 63–70.

p. 12/13 Peter Haberl is a sport psychology consultant at the United States Olympic Training Center in Colorado Springs. He is continuing his work with the United States Women's National Ice Hockey program. Mary Turco is the author of *Crashing the Net: The U.S. Women's Olympic Ice Hockey Team and the Road to the Gold* (New York: Harper Perennial, 1999).

p. 14/15 John Cortlett's presentation is included in the "Proceedings of the Fourteenth Annual Conference on Counseling Athletes," Springfield College, May 1998.

p. 16   The North American Indian Traveling College authored and published *Tewaarthon: Akwesasne's Story of Our National Game* in 1978. The reference is to page 2.

Chapter 2

p. 24　Kevin Ryan and Karen Bohlin, *Building Character in Schools: Practical Ways to Bring Moral Instruction to Life* (San Francisco: Jossey-Bass, 1999).

p. 25　Russell Gough, *Character Is Everything : Promoting Ethical Excellence in Sports* (Fort Worth, TX: Harcourt Brace, 1997).

p. 35/36 Steve Tigner's version of "Aristotle's Six Moral States" is presented in the course, Cultural Foundations for Educators 1, at Boston University. The figure can be found in his course packet, *Outlines and Reading Aids for Aristotle's Nichomachean Ethics* (1994).

p. 38/39 Ken Dryden authored the report, *Evaluation of Aigles Bleus' Hockey Program* (Universite DeMoncton, June 1996).

p. 40　Jeff Beedy presented at the plenary session at the Reclaiming the Purpose of Sport conference, Boston University, November 1998.

p. 41/42 See E.J. Delattre, "Teaching Integrity: The Boundaries of Moral Education," *Education Week*, Vol. 48 (1990), pp. 1–4.

p. 41　H.S. Glenn and J. S. Warner, *Developing Capable Young People* (Hurst, Texas: Humansphere, Inc., 1984).

p. 44/45 L. Yearly, *Mencius and Aquinas: Theories of Virtue and Conceptions of Courage* (Albany, NY: State University of New York Press, 1990).

p. 47　R. Wuthnow, *Acts of Compassion* (Princeton, NJ: Princeton University Press, 1991).

p. 47/48 Peter Haberl is a sport psychology consultant at the United States Olympic Training Center in Colorado Springs. He is continuing his work with the United States Women's National Ice Hockey program. Mary Turco is the author of *Crashing the Net: The U.S. Women's Olympic Ice Hockey Team and the Road to the Gold* (New York: Harper Perennial, 1999).

p. 49   T. Sizer, *Horace's School: Redesigning the American High School* (Boston: Houghton Mifflin,1992), p. 74.

Chapter 3

p. 51   Steven Tigner's "Educator's Affirmation" is cited in Kevin Ryan and James Cooper, *Those Who Can, Teach,* 7th Edition (Boston: Houghton-Mifflin, 1995).

p. 52   The quote is from Marianne Williamson's book, *A Return to Love: Reflections on the Principles of a Course in Miracles* (New York: HarperCollins, 1996).

p. 53   John Dewey, *Democracy and Education* (New York: The Free Press, 1916)

p. 54/55 M. Boyea, *Elements of Sport Leadership: A Comparison of High School Boy's Basketball Coaches with Varying Won-Loss Records,* unpublished doctoral dissertation, University of Maryland, 1994.

p. 56   G.D. Wright, *Analysis of Qualities Essential for a Superior College Coach,* unpublished doctoral dissertation, Boston University, 1998.

p. 57   John Dewey, *Democracy and Education* (New York: The Free Press, 1916), p.31.

p. 58   The *Internalizing Virtue Model* was developed by Kevin Ryan, Karen Bohlin, and Deborah Farmer of Boston University's Center for the Advancement of Ethics and Character.

p. 61   R. Kegan, *The Evolving Self* (Cambridge, MA: Harvard University Press, 1983).

p. 62   Sam Osherson was a keynote speaker at the Spring 1999 Independent School Health Association (ISHA) conference at Phillips Exeter Academy. He is the author of "The Art of Mentoring," published in the Fall 1999 *ISHA Newsletter.*

p. 62/63 Carol Hotchkiss was a keynote speaker at the Spring 1999 Independent School Health Association (ISHA) conference at Phillips Exeter Academy.

p. 63/64 M. Harris, "I've Got a Name: The Power of Student Naming," unpublished manuscript, Boston University School of Education, 1998.

p. 64   R. Wuthnow, *Acts of Compassion* (Princeton, NJ: Princeton University Press, 1991).

p. 64   G.A. Larson, "In Defense of the Generalist: The Vital Role of the Teacher/Coach," *Independent School,* Fall 1996, pp. 22–27.

p. 68   S. Tigner, "Souls in Conflict," *Journal for a Just and Caring Education,* Vol 2, No. 4, pp. 349–359.

p. 69/70 See the *Springfield College Triangle,* Fall 1998.

Chapter 4

p. 79   See C.A. Bartlett and S. Ghoshal, "Changing the Role of Top Management: Beyond Systems to People," *Harvard Business Review,* May/June 1995, pp. 132–142.

p. 84   Erik H. Erikson, *Youth: Identity and Crisis* (New York: W.W. Norton, 1994).

p. 90   R. Kegan, *The Evolving Self* (Cambridge, MA: Harvard University Press, 1983).

Chapter 5

p. 92/93 For more classical and reflective reading see Plato, *Republic,* Grube's translation as revised by C.D.C. Reeve (Indianapolis, IN: Hackett Publishers, 1992).

p. 93/95 Ronald A. Smith *Sports and Freedom: The Rise of Big-Time College Athletics* (Oxford University Press, 1990).

Chapter 6

p. 113   See E.J. Delattre, "Teaching Integrity: The Boundaries of Moral Education," *Education Week,* Vol. 48 (1990), pp. 1–4.

Chapter 7

p. 130 Lisa Lahey's "Generalizations about Teacher Evaluation" was presented at St. Paul's School, Concord, NH, 1990.

p. 131/132 M. Walker Buckalew has created a unique teacher evaluation process as described in *Meaningful Faculty Evaluation* (Wilmington, DE: Strategic Performance Designs, Inc. and Nashville, TN: Francis Communications, Inc.).

p. 134/135 M.W. Berkowitz and the Character Education Partnership Assessment Committee, *A Primer for Evaluating A Character Education Initiative* (Washington, DC: The Character Education Partnership, 1999).

p. 137–139 The Leader-Detractor scale can be found in J.P. Beedy, *Sports Plus: Developing Youth Sports Programs that Teach Positive Values* (Hamilton, MA: Project Adventure, 1997), pp. 42–45.

Chapter 8

p.143 Keynote address by Dr. Peter Greer, Headmaster of The Montclair Kimberley Academy, at the "Reclaiming the Purpose of Sport" conference, Montclair, NJ, November 1999.

p. 144/145 For a more comprehensive view of the flow model, see M. Csikszentmihalyi, *Flow: The Psychology of Optimal Experience* (New York: HarperCollins, 1990).

p. 147/148 The Factors of Skilled Performance figure was created by Leonard D. Zaichkowsky, professor of education at Boston University and Gerald A. Larson, head of school, Cheshire Academy. *Physical, Motor and Fitness Development in Children and Adolescents.*

p. 148/149 M. Gladwell, "The Physical Genius," *The New Yorker*, August 2, 1999, pp. 57–65.

p. 156 For more information on performance excellence, see Terry Orlick's *In Pursuit of Excellence : How to Win in Sport and Life Through Mental Training*. 3rd Edition. Champaign, IL: Human Kinetics, 2000)

p. 158 S. Ungerleider, *Mental Training for Peak Performance: Top Athletes Reveal the Mind Exercises they use to Excel* (Emmaus, PA: Rodale Press, 1996).

p. 157 L. Hardy, G Jones, & D. Gould, *Understanding Psychological Preparation for Sport: Theory and Practice of Elite Performers.* (New York: Wiley and Sons, 1996).

p. 158/159 A. Bandura, *Self-efficacy: The Exercise of Control* (New York: W. H. Freeman, 1997), pp. 391–392.

p. 160 For more information on performance excellence, see Yuri Hanin's *Emotions in Sport* (Champaign, IL: Human Kinetics, 1999).

p. 161 The "Zones of Optimal Performance" illustration is an adaptation from D. M. Landers and S.H. Boutcher, "Arousal Performance Relationships," in *Applied Sport Psychology—Personal Growth to Peak Performance,* Jean Williams, Ed. (Mountain View, CA: Mayfield Publishing), p. 207.

p. 163 G. S. Hamill, "Psychological and Physiological Correlates of the Individual Zones of Optimal Functioning," doctoral dissertation, Boston University, 1996.

Chapter 9

p. 166 See "The Second Quarter: How Children Learn" in Jeff Beedy's *Sports Plus: Developing Youth Sports Programs that Teach Positive Values* (Hamilton, MA: Project Adventure, 1997), pp. 61–89.

p. 167 See J. O. Prochaska, C.C. DiClemente, J.C. and Norcross, "In Search of How People Change: Applications to Addictive Behaviors," *The American Psychologist,* Vol. 47, No. 9, pp. 1102–1114.

p. 170 Lou Nanni, the executive assistant to the president of the University of Notre Dame, keynoted *Service as Privilege,* at The Culver Academies, Culver, Indiana on September 28, 2000.

Suggested Readings

Beedy, Jeffrey, Zierk, Tom, & Gough, Russell. *Effective Guidelines for Character Education through Sports*. Washington, DC: Character Education Partnership, 2000.

Beedy, Jeffrey Pratt. *Sports Plus: Developing Youth Sports Program that Teach Positive Values*. Hamilton, MA: Project Adventure, 1997.

Clifford, Craig & Feezell, Randolph M. *Coaching for Character—Reclaiming the Principles of Sportsmanship*. Champaign, IL: Human Kinetics, 1997.

Gough, Russell W. *Character Is Everything—Promoting Ethical Excellence in Sports*. Fort Worth, TX: Harcourt Press, 1997.

Lumpkin, Angela; Stoll, Sharon Kay; and Beller, Jennifer, M. *Sport Ethics: Applications for Fair Play*. Second edition. Dubuque, IA: McGraw-Hill, 1999.

Murphy, Shane. *The Cheers and Tears—A Healthy Alternative to the Dark Side of Youth Sports Today*. San Francisco: Jossey-Bass, 1999.

Shields, David Lyle Light, & Bredemeier, Brenda Jo Light (1995). *Character Development and Physical Activity*. Champaign, IL: Human Kinetics, 1995.

Thompson, Jim. *Positive Coaching: Building Character and Self-esteem Through Sports*. Portola Valley, CA: Warde Publishers, 1995.

Character and Sport Organizations

The Center for Character Education at The Culver Academies
Attn: John Yeager—Box 72
1300 Academy Road
Culver, Indiana 46511
(219) 842–8159
www.culver.org

Positive Learning Using Sports
PO Box 219
New Hampton, NH 03256
(603) 744–5401
plusinfor@sportsplus.org
www.sportsplus.org

Positive Coaching Alliance
Department of Athletics
Stanford University
Stanford, CA 94305–6150
650.725.0024 (telephone)
650.725.7242 (fax)
pca@positivecoach.org
www.positivecoach.org

MomsTeam, Inc.
60 Thoreau Street
Suite 288
Concord, MA 01742
www.momsteam.com

Center for Sport, Character & Culture
University of Notre Dame
Note Dame, IN46556
219/631-4445
email: cscc@nd.edu

National Alliance For Youth Sports
2050 Vista Parkway
West Palm Beach, FL 33411
(561) 684-1141 *Fax (561)* 684-2546
(800) 729-2057
(800) 688-KIDS
nays@nays.org

The Character Education Partnership
1600 K Street, NW Suite 501
Washington, DC 20006
202/296/7743
www.character.org

The Center for the Advancement of Ethics and Character
Boston University
605 Commonwealth Ave.
Boston, MA 02215
(617) 353-3262
www.bu.edu/education/centersresources/centeradvethicschar

Resources available from
National Professional Resources, Inc.
(Books & Videos)

Beane, Allan L. *The Bully Free Classroom: Over 100 Tips and Strategies for Teachers K-8*. Minneapolis, MN: Free Spirit Publishing, 1999. $19.95

Beedy, Jeffrey. *Sports Plus: Developing Youth Sports Programs that Teach Positive Values*. Hamilton, MA: Project Adventure, Inc., 1997. $16.00

Begun, Ruth W. *Ready-to-Use Social Skills Lesson (4 levels: Pre K-K; 1–3; 4–6; 7–12)* West Nyack, NY: Center for Applied Research, 1995. $29.95 each

Benson, Peter L., Galbraith, Judy, & Espeland, Pamela. *What Teens Need To Succeed*. Minneapolis, MN: Free Spirit Press, 1998. $14.95

Block, Martin. *A Teachers Guide to Including Students with Disabilities in General Physical Education Programs*. Brookes Publishing, 2000. $44.95

Bocchino, Rob. *Emotional Literacy: To Be a Different Kind of Smart*. Thousand Oaks, CA: Corwin Press, 1999. $24.95

Character Connections Monthly Newsletter. Port Chester, NY: National Professional Resources (Publisher). $99.00 yearly subscription

Christesen, Mirka. *Character Kaleidoscope*. Port Chester, NY: National Professional Resources, 2000. $29.95

Cohen, Jonathan. *Educating Minds & Hearts*. New York, NY: Teacher's College Press, 1999. $21.95

Csikszentmihalyi, Mihaly. *Finding Flow*. New York, NY: Basic Books, 1997. $13.00

Dotson, Anne C., & Dotson, Karen D. *Teaching Character/Teacher's Guide*. Chapel Hill, NC: Character Development Publishing, 1997. $24.95

Garbarino, James. *Lost Boys*. New York, NY: The Free Press, 1999. $25.00

Girard, Kathryn & Koch, Susan J. *Conflict Resolution in the Schools: A Manual for Educators*. San Francisco, CA: Jossey-Bass, 1996. $35.00

Glasser, William. *Building A Quality School: A Matter of Responsibility* (Video). Port Chester, NY: National Professional Resources, 1998. $99.00

Glasser, William. *Choice Theory*. New York, NY: Harper Collins, 1998. $23.00

Goleman, Daniel. *Emotional Intelligence: A New Vision For Educators* (Video). Port Chester, NY: National Professional Resources, 1996. $89.95

Goleman, Daniel. *Emotional Intelligence: Why It Can Matter More Than IQ*. New York, NY: Bantam Books, 1995. $13.95

Harris, Pat, et al. *Character Education: Application in the Classroom, Secondary Edition* (Video). Port Chester, NY: National Professional Resources, 1998. $89.95

Kagan, Spencer. *Building Character Through Cooperative Learning* (Video). Port Chester, NY: National Professional Resources, 1999. $99.99

Kagan, Laurie, et al. *Teambuilding*. San Clemente, CA: Kagan Cooperative Learning, 1997. $25.00

Kohn, Alfie. *Punished By Rewards*. New York, NY: Houghton Mifflin Co., 1998. $13.95

Lickona, Thomas et al. *Character Education: Restoring Respect & Responsibility in Our Schools* (Video). Port Chester, NY: National Professional Resources, 1996. $79.95

Lickona, Thomas. *Educating for Character: How Our Schools Can Teach Respect & Responsibilty*. New York, NY: Bantam Books, 1994. $14.95

Macan, Lynn, et al. *Character Education: Application in the Classroom, Elementary Edition* (Video). Port Chester, NY: National Professional Resources, 1998. $89.95

McKay, Linda et al. *Service Learning: Curriculum, Standards and the Community* (Video). Port Chester, NY: National Professional Resources, 1998. $99.00

Packer, Alex, J. *How Rude! The Teenager's Guide to Good Manners, Proper Behavior*

And Not Grossing People Out. Minneapolis, MN: Free Spirit Publishing, 1997 $19.95

Perlstein, Ruth & Thrall, Gloria. *Ready-to-Use Conflict Resolution Activities for Secondary Students.* West Nyack, NY: Center for Applied Research in Education, 1996. $29.95

Pert, Candace. *Emotion: Gatekeeper to Performance—The Mind/Body Connection*

(Video). Port Chester, NY: National Professional Resources, 1999. $99.00

Pollack, William. *Real Boys.* New York, NY: Henry Holt & Co., 1999. $13.95

Renzulli, Joseph. *Developing the Gifts & Talents of ALL Students* (Video). Port Chester, NY: National Professional Resources, 1999. $99.95

Salovey, Peter et al. *Optimizing Intelligences: Thinking, Emotion & Creativity* (Video). Port Chester, NY: National Professional Resources, 1998. $99.95

Scully, Jennifer. *The Power of Social Skills in Character Development: Helping Diverse Learners Succeed.* Port Chester, NY: National Professional Resources, 2000. $29.95

Sizer, Ted. *Crafting of America's Schools* (Video). Port Chester, NY: National Professional Resources, 1997. $99.95

Stirling, Diane, Archibald, Georgia, McKay, Linda & Berg, Shelley. *Character Education Connections for School, Home and Community.* Port Chester, NY: National Professional Resources, 2000. $39.95

Teele, Sue. *Rainbows of Intelligence: Raising Student Performance Through Multiple Intelligence* (video). Port Chester, NY: National Professional Resources, 1999. $99.95

Teolis, Beth. *Ready-to-Use Conflict Resolution Activities, Elementary Edition*. West Nyack, NY: Center for Applied Research in Education, 1998. $29.95

ALL BOOKS & VIDEOS AVAILABLE FOR PURCHASE FROM
NATIONAL PROFESSIONAL RESOURCES
1-800-453-7461

For additional current resources, see our web site
www.nprinc.com

The Authors

John M. Yeager is the director of Character, Sport and Health at The Culver Academies in Culver, Indiana. He is a consultant to Boston University's Center for the Advancement of Ethics and Character where he formerly was an associate scholar and clinical assistant professor in BU's School of Education. He had more than twelve years of teaching and coaching experience in public schools before coming to Boston University in 1988. Dr. Yeager consults with schools and colleges on the nature of character and sport. He has also played and coached at the secondary school, college, club, and professional levels. In 1996, he was inducted into the New England Lacrosse Hall of Fame.

Amy L. Baltzell is a clinical assistant professor in the School of Education at Boston University. She is also a performance-enhancement consultant who has conducted applied sport performance interventions with more than sixty elite, collegiate, club, and youth teams and consulted with more than 150 individual collegiate, elite, and professional athletes. Dr. Baltzell was a member of the 1992 USA Olympic Rowing Team and a crew member of *America³*, the first all-woman America's Cup Sailing Team. She has coached women's crew at Radcliffe College.

John N. Buxton is the head of The Culver Educational Foundation in Culver, Indiana. His interest in character and sport has evolved from his service as an independent school administrator, educator and coach for twenty-nine years. He was also a three-sport athlete at Brown University. He is currently a doctoral candidate in the Department of Administration, Training, and Policy Studies at the Boston University School of Education.

Wallace B. Bzdell is an assistant director of the Archer Center for Student Leadership Development and class instructor at Rensselaer Polytechnic Institute. Previously, he was the assistant director of student-athlete support services at Northeastern University. A former junior and college hockey player, Mr. Bzdell consults with numerous organizations, athletes, and coaches on mental toughness training for performance enhancement; including the Union College athletic department. He also consults/lectures with the Massachusetts Youth Hockey and USA Hockey Coach Education Programs. Mr. Bzdell is a doctoral candidate in counseling psychology, specializing in sport psychology, at the Boston University School of Education.

Major Contributors

Mark J. Boyea is the director of athletics at The Montclair Kimberley Academy (MKA) in Montclair, New Jersey. Over his twenty-year career, Dr. Boyea has been a highly successful college coach and athletics administrator, private school athletics administrator, and sport psychologist. Prior to arriving at MKA, he was commissioner of the Washington (DC) Catholic Athletic Conference, one of the premier high school athletic associations in the nation. He is also MKA's varsity girl's basketball coach.

Eric Hartung is a research assistant with the New England Research Institute. He has coached and played at the high school and college levels and is currently an assistant coach with Harvard University's men's lacrosse team. He is a doctoral candidate in the curriculum and teaching department in the Boston University School of Education.

Photo Credit: Boston University Photo Services